PHILOSOPHY FOR TEENS

PHILOSOPHY FOR TEENS

QUESTIONING LIFE'S BIG IDEAS

SHARON M. KAYE, PH.D., & PAUL THOMSON, PH.D.

ILLUSTRATED BY JON COMPTON

PRUFROCK PRESS INC.
WACO, TX

Library of Congress Cataloging-in-Publication Data

Kaye, Sharon M.
Philosophy for teens : questioning life's big ideas / Sharon M. Kaye and Paul Thomson.
p. cm.
ISBN-13: 978-1-59363-202-1 (pbk.)
ISBN-10: 1-59363-202-9 (pbk.)
1. Philosophy. I. Thomson, Paul. II. Title.
BD31.K28 2006
100—dc22
2006019570

Edited by Lacy Elwood
Cover and Layout Design by Marjorie Parker
Illustrations by Jon Compton

ISBN-13: 978-1-59363-202-1
ISBN-10: 1-59363-202-9

Prufrock Press Inc.
P.O. Box 8813
Waco, TX 76714-8813
Phone: (800) 998-2208
Fax: (800) 240-0333
http://www.prufrock.com

For Tris and Robin with love

TABLE OF CONTENTS

Teacher's Guide xiii
Introduction 1

PART 1: BEAUTY

Chapter 1: What Is Love? 7
Chapter 2: Is Beauty a Matter of Fact or a Matter of Taste? 15
Chapter 3: What Is the Purpose of Art? 23
Chapter 4: Is There a Difference Between Health and Beauty? 31

PART 2: TRUTH

Chapter 5: Is There Anything That Cannot Be True? 43
Chapter 6: Is Lying Always Wrong? 51
Chapter 7: Does Every Question Have an Answer? 59
Chapter 8: Should We Accept Reality? 69

PART 3: JUSTICE

Chapter 9: What is Discrimination? 81
Chapter 10: Do Animals Have Rights? 91
Chapter 11: Who Will Take Care of the Environment? 101
Chapter 12: What Would Happen if There Were No Governments? 109

PART 4: GOD

Chapter 13: Why Do Bad Things Happen to Good People? 119
Chapter 14: What Is the Meaning of Life? 127

Appendix A: Dialogue Worksheet 137
Appendix B: The Trial and Death of Socrates, and Plato's Theory of Forms 139
Appendix C: Empiricism 145
Glossary 149
About the Authors 152

LIST OF THOUGHT EXPERIMENTS

Thought Experiment: The Replacement Brother 11
Thought Experiment: Seeing Beauty 18
Thought Experiment: The Nature of Art 28
Thought Experiment: Just the Way You Are 35
Thought Experiment: The Mob and the Scapegoat 54
Thought Experiment: Time Traveling Yourself Out of Existence 63
Thought Experiment: Getting Your Jollies 75
Thought Experiment: Desert Dessert 85
Thought Experiment: The Grandchildren That Never Were 104
Thought Experiment: An Island of Your Very Own 113
Thought Experiment: The Next Dr. Frankenstein 122
Thought Experiment: The Most Important Choice of All 132

PREFACE

Welcome to *Philosophy for Teens*, a book about values focused on aesthetics and ethics. This volume is arranged topically rather than historically in order to emphasize the connection between ideas. We have, however, included relevant historical details offset from the main text.

Each chapter opens with a casual and realistic dialogue between two fictional teenagers who disagree about something (e.g., over whether lying is always wrong or about what love is). Their disagreement illustrates two philosophical positions on an issue, setting up the topic for the chapter. In each chapter we explore two or more sides of a classical philosophical debate. The debate always includes a "thought experiment" to test the more controversial claims. At the end of each chapter are discussion questions, exercises, activities, community action steps, and references for further reading. Our goal is to bring philosophy alive through active learning.

We hope you enjoy reading this book as much as we enjoyed writing it! Please feel free to contact us with comments and suggestions.

Sharon Kaye (skaye@jcu.edu)
Paul Thomson (thomson@jcu.edu)

ACKNOWLEDGEMENTS

This project began life as the textbook we use for teaching in the Carroll-Cleveland Philosophers' Program at John Carroll University in Cleveland, OH. This program brings students from the Cleveland Municipal School District to our campus once a week for a philosophy, service learning, and enrichment class. We are the instructors for the philosophy part of the curriculum. Drafts of this book have been used in the program many times, and we think that this has resulted in a well-tested final product. We would like to thank all of the people who helped launch this project. There are too many to mention by name.

We give special thanks to: Dr. Jenifer Merritt, founder and director of the Carroll-Cleveland Philosophers' Program; Ms. Roslyn Smith-Crumb, operations director, 2004–2005; municipal students and teachers who participated in the Carroll-Cleveland Philosophers' Program; our John Carroll University undergraduate teaching assistants in the program—Dan Matusicky, Lauren Stockhausen, Linda Kawentel, Rhiannon Lathy, Taleiza Calloway, Brittany McClane, Zach Miller, Mary Garrety, Alex Decker, Jon Sopko, Dan Marangoni, Sahar Shouman, Betsy Rafferty, Marie Semple, and Robert Kumazec; Tim Weidel, philosophy work-study student who helped us format the text and the glossary; Marc Engel, Shaker Heights High School student who proofed the penultimate draft; Eileen Murphy, secretary of our department; and our fellow faculty members.

We would also like to give special thanks to John Carroll University for research leave during the spring of 2006 and for its generous support of the Carroll-Cleveland Philosophers' Program.

TEACHER'S GUIDE

Although this book can be read on its own, it is especially useful in the classroom. We have implemented it with success in a wide variety of settings: from special classes with 50 teens and 10 teaching assistants, to standard classes with 25 teens and 1 teacher, to occasional workshops with 10 co-learners of different ages.

The authors have designed each chapter to be taught in one session. Of course, ideally, the students would read the chapter on their own prior to class. Because the chapters are fun and accessible, this is a reasonable assignment. Nevertheless, we often proceed, and proceed fruitfully, without assigning any homework at all. When the authors have a 2-hour time block, a typical class period goes as follows: (1) We introduce the central question featured in the chapter; (2) We do a dramatic reading of the opening dialogue; (3) We write answers to the questions at the end of the dialogue; (4) We discuss highlights from the chapter (this may involve reading sections of text out loud together); (5) We write dialogues in small groups; and (6) We perform the dialogues for the class and share our reactions. When we have just a 1-hour time block we simply eliminate steps 5 and 6 or continue with those steps at the next class meeting. In courses that include steps 5 and 6, we often make a video of the best dialogues for the students to watch together on the last day of class and, if copies can be made, to take home as a special memento.

Teachers, you should be aware that the Activities section of each chapter contains an idea for a film students can watch that relates to the topic at hand. Please note that some of these movies are rated R, for some mature content. You should always check your school's guidelines and gain parental permission before allowing your students to view the film. Asking a student's parent(s) for permission, or suggesting parents view the film with their child, is a good way to communicate about the philosophical ideals that the students are learning. You should always watch the film on your own before showing it to students, and consider if you should show the film in its entirety or just show particular scenes that convey the chapter's topics well. Remember: It's always best to err on the side of caution.

Our students deeply enjoy the performance aspect of our "drama pedagogy"—to such an extent that dialogue production can begin to take over the class. The perennial issues discussed in each chapter have a way of fanning the flames of their creative energy. We recommend adhering to a schedule and keeping dialogues short to allow plenty of time to share reactions. We have developed a dialogue worksheet to facilitate this process (see Appendix A at the back of this book). The worksheet assigns clear roles to each of the students and brings the purpose of their performance into focus. Drama provides rare opportunities for self-transformation. Having witnessed these in our classroom time and again, we deem the effort well worth it.

The educational standards addressed by the book include history, English, and science. The exercises are designed to improve general literacy along with written and oral communication skills. The chapters need not be read in succession, as the content of each is independent of the others. Teachers can make this book the basis for a full course in philosophy or introduce relevant chapters into other preexisting courses. For example, a history class studying the ancient world would benefit from Chapters 1–3 and Chapter 8, which feature Plato, Socrates, Aristotle, and the Stoics, respectively. Chapters 6 and 7 correspond to works of literature commonly studied in English classes. A science class would find value in Chapter 4, which discusses health, and Chapter 11, which discusses the environment. Furthermore, any of the chapters would enhance dialogue work in a drama class. We have found the book to be highly adaptable to different learning environments, helping students think about old subjects in new ways.

This book enables teachers to assess students in multiple dimensions through written work, oral performance, and group projects. Because there are no right or wrong answers in philosophy, it can be a difficult subject to grade. In fact, the teacher's main responsibility is to encourage students to explore and be respectful of a wide variety of opinions. However, written work (whether this be answers to questions in the book or a running free-form philosophy journal) can be graded for excellence of expression. We recommend requiring the students to turn in some written work at the end of each class to receive written feedback whether or not a grade is recorded. A point system for class participation may also be useful to reward quality contributions and cooperation. Students should come away from the course (or course unit) understanding the importance of clear thinking and communication. They will be excited to discover that human beings have been wondering about the same things they have for a very long time. In our experience, this excitement translates into leaps and bounds of learning.

INTRODUCTION

Do you ever think about weird things?

For example, have you ever wondered whether everyone else sees colors the same way as you? What if they all see grass and trees as purple, even though they call it "green"? How would you ever know?

Have you ever wondered what animals would say if they could talk? Maybe they would talk just like us about everything happening around them. Or, maybe they don't understand what's happening and therefore wouldn't have anything to say even if they could talk.

Have you ever wondered what would happen if all of the world's problems were suddenly solved? Would people's hair stop turning gray? Would we be happy? Would we get bored and demand to have our problems back?

Maybe you've never really thought about things like that before. But, if you have, you're not the only one. These thoughts aren't really weird, they're philosophical, and that is what this book is about.

Philosophical thinking is good for you. Some people like it and some people don't, but everyone should learn how to do it, because philosophy helps you figure out what life is all about. It helps you come to understand what living a good life might mean, and it helps you answer tough questions about who you are.

When you think about what colors look like to other people, you're considering what it's like to see things from someone else's point of view. We all get along better if we remind ourselves that not everyone sees things the same way. Likewise, when you form an opinion about how animals would talk, you're also forming an opinion about how they should be treated. Everyone needs to decide for him- or herself just how much respect we owe to our fellow creatures. Most importantly, when we dream about a perfect world, we give ourselves motivation for improvement. It feels good to know that things don't have to stay as they are if we don't want them to.

So, what do we want from life, how should we interact with others, and what is life all about? People disagree about the answers to these questions. The goal of philosophy is not to identify final answers that everyone should accept, but to explore different answers. Because it's extremely unlikely that *you* are the only person who has the correct belief about every philosophical question, it is important to take a critical attitude about all philosophical positions. In most subjects, such as math, history, and science, there are right answers and wrong answers. The textbook contains the facts and the teacher corrects errors. For the most part, philosophy is not like that. There are no philosophical facts. Everyone has the right to disagree and develop his or her own philosophical ideas.

In addition to introducing you to a number of important philosophical concepts, a central aim of this book is to show that disagreements need not be a bad thing. Most people don't like to disagree. Two reactions are common: They either lash out or shut down. These reactions are unfortunate, because a disagreement is an excellent opportunity for personal growth.

Philosophers actually like disagreement. How else will you ever break out of the rut in your own mind and discover which of your opinions are worth having? How else will you keep your wits sharp? In order to stay fresh and alive you have to shake things up a little bit from time to time! There's no better way to shake yourself up than to listen to someone with opinions that differ from yours. And, when we say *listen*, we mean actually listen. This doesn't mean just letting them talk. Nor does it mean accepting whatever they say. It means hearing what they have to say and trying to understand their point of view and then deciding for yourself. It's a simple thing . . . but it's huge.

In this book we look at a number of controversial opinions on interesting topics related to values. By studying a variety of perspectives, you should come to understand and express your own perspective better. As with all things, this is easier to do if you're having fun.

It's fun to experiment with new ideas, even though it may feel strange at first. We begin each chapter of this book with an exercise to help you get the hang of it. The exercise involves reading a dialogue between two fictional high school students and answering some questions about it. We encourage you to read the dialogues out loud with someone else, each of you adopting the role of one of the characters. Try to put yourself in your character's mind frame and see what it might be like to actually hold the view he or she advocates. You may decide you agree, or you may decide you disagree. Either way, if you have entertained the view as your own, it will be easier for you to give reasons for your decision. At the end of each chapter, we challenge you to write a dialogue of your own on one of the themes discussed.

Somewhere in the middle of each chapter you will find another type of exercise known as a "thought experiment." A thought experiment is an imaginary scenario designed to test the truth of a controversial claim. For example, suppose someone makes the claim that religion is a necessary feature of society. We could test this claim by trying to imagine a society that functions without religion. If we can imagine this, then the original claim is false. If we cannot imagine it, then the claim stands as a reasonable possibility. At the end of each chapter, we challenge you to construct a thought experiment to test one of the central claims made in the chapter.

Keep in mind that any book referred to in the text will be listed at the end of the chapter in the References section. You will also find a list of books and articles related to each chapter in the section marked Further Reading. These lists will enable you to pursue issues that interest you on your own. The discussion questions at the end of each chapter are designed to enhance your understanding of the concepts presented in the chapter, while the activities and community action steps are designed to help you apply these concepts to your daily life. Finally, there is a glossary at the end of the book to help you keep track of new philosophical terms.

Philosophy wakes you up and makes you think. Once you get used to it, you won't know how you ever lived without it.

PART 1

Beauty

La Gue, 1895, William Bouguereau

CHAPTER 1
What Is Love?

The Photograph

Matt and Jen are two old friends having lunch together. As they are finishing, Matt pulls a photograph out of his wallet.

MATT: Well, here she is, Jen. <*He proudly hands the picture to her.*> My new girlfriend, Shawna. Isn't she beautiful?

JEN: <*Glances disinterestedly at the photo.*> How could I tell whether or not she's beautiful from an image?

MATT: What do you mean? <*He snatches back the photograph.*> It's a great picture. You're just jealous 'cause I'm in love.

JEN: Yeah, right. I'm actually making a point, OK? Beauty isn't something you can see on the outside. It's in a person's soul. I'd have to know Shawna to be able to tell whether or not she's beautiful.

MATT: Well, then take my word for it, hon. <*Leaning back in his chair and smiling broadly, he ticks off each item on his fingers as he continues.*> She's attractive, she has a good job, she's a great dancer, and she makes everyone laugh. How could you not love a woman like that? I'm telling you, this is the real thing.

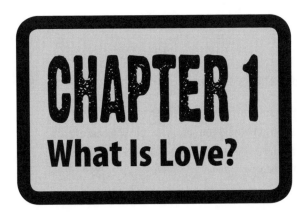

JEN: Matthew, Matthew, Matthew. <*She shakes her head.*> True love isn't about checking off items on a list. If Shawna gets laid off from work and runs out of good jokes, you're not gonna love her anymore? And, what if she's in an accident that scars her face and leaves her crippled? Are you gonna dump her for some other cute dancer?

MATT: Whoa! Those are some pretty awful prospects that I don't need to be worrying about. But, I will say this. Beauty *must* be something you see on the outside because otherwise people would never fall in love. Haven't you ever heard of love at first *sight*? How do you explain that? Some kind of soul radar? *<Matt wiggles his fingers over his head like antennae to poke fun at her view.>*

JEN: Come on! There are a lot of different kinds of love. I know *you* have a soul, because you've changed a lot on the outside since we became friends, but you're still the same person that I love.

MATT: Oh, man! Let's not get all mushy now. *<Matt makes a face.>*

Questions:

- Why does Jen think beauty is something you cannot see? Why does Matt think you can see it? With whom do you agree more, and why?
- Describe someone you think is beautiful. Do you think this person is beautiful because of the qualities you described or because of something else?
- Describe someone you love. If someone asked you why you love this person, what would you say?
- Explain the difference between romantic love and friendly love.

What Is Love?

People say love makes the world go around. Almost every song on the radio is about love, and most of the movies we enjoy involve a love story. But, how many people stop to ask themselves what exactly love is? Philosophers are the ones who ask questions about things everyone else takes for granted. Love is something human beings have been taking for granted since the beginning of recorded history. Philosophers have been trying to figure out what it is for at least as long.

Plato explored the nature of love in his dialogue, *Symposium*. It portrays a group of people at a party, each one presenting a theory on what love is. One of the men, a playwright named Aristophanes, argues that true love means you have found your "other half." He tells everyone at the party that human beings were originally created in three different ways: (1) with both a male and a female half, (2) with two male halves, or (3) with two female halves. One of the gods became angry with humans, however, and split the halves apart, scattering them in every direction. Aristophanes suggests we should all devote our lives to finding our long lost other half. We'll recognize our other half when we see it, because it was once part of us. Our other half is our true love.

Perhaps Aristophanes does not mean for us to take his story as literally true, but rather as a metaphor for the good feelings we have when we are in love.

While philosophers agree that love is good, they disagree over why it's good. According to Plato, love is good because it is *rational*, meaning that there are reasons for it. He believed true love is always directed toward true beauty. True beauty is not something you see or feel. Rather, you come to know it exists by doing philosophy—that is, by thinking about it.

Plato argued that when you see something that strikes you as beautiful, you are really just seeing a partial reflection of true beauty, just as a painting or even a photograph only captures part of the real thing. True beauty, or what Plato calls the Form of Beauty, has no particular color, shape, or size. Rather, it is an abstract idea, like the number five. You can make drawings of the number five in blue or red ink, big or small, but the number five itself is none of those things. *Abstract ideas* are objects of thought that have no physical form. Think of the abstract idea of a triangle. Although it has no particular color or size, it somehow lies within each and every triangle you see. Plato thought the same

Plato (427–347 BC) was a philosopher who lived in Ancient Greece, in Athens. He was one of the first philosophers in Western history to record his philosophical ideas in a systematic way and he was immensely influential to the field of philosophy. He opened a school for philosophers in Athens called The Academy, which gave rise to our word *academic*. Plato's most widely read work is *Apology*, an account of the trial of his teacher Socrates. In other works Plato investigated the concepts of such things as piety, virtue, the nature of justice, the nature of love, and the possibility of life after death, to name but a few. Plato wrote his philosophy books in the form of dialogues, much like the ones at the beginning of each chapter in this book. Why do you think he wrote this way?

was true of beauty. The Form of Beauty somehow lies within each and every beautiful thing you see.

According to Plato, when you love someone, you actually love the Form of Beauty that you see reflected within that person. Because the Form of Beauty is the highest good, we have every reason to love it.

In an ancient poem called *The Odyssey*, Homer tells the story of a man named Odysseus and his wife Penelope. Odysseus and Penelope are very much in love. Then, one day Odysseus is called away to the Trojan War. Because he is gone for a long time, everyone assumes he is dead, and they demand that Penelope remarry. Men come from far and wide, each one claiming to be just as good as Odysseus. Penelope rejects every one of them. Soon a mysterious stranger comes along who really is just as good as Odysseus at everything. Fortunately for Penelope, the man turns out to be the long lost Odysseus himself, in disguise. What do you think Homer is trying to say about love in this story?

Penelope and the Suitors, 1912, by John William Waterhouse

The claim that love is rational has an interesting implication, however. If you see more beauty in person A than you see in person B, then you should love person A more than you love person B. If you see the same amount of beauty in two different people, then you should love them the same amount.

Michel de Montaigne (1533–1592) was a French philosopher who disagreed with Plato. According to Montaigne, true love is *irrational,* meaning that there is no reason for it. He argued that love is at its best when it is maximally free, meaning not limited by any constraint, including reason. There is no way to explain or justify your feelings. If you truly love someone, you will never know exactly why.

Montaigne believed this account of true love especially applies to close friendships. Ask yourself this question: Why do you have the friends you have? You might say, "Because I like them." But, now ask yourself a further question: Why do you like them? You might be tempted to answer, "I just do." Montaigne said the same thing. Speaking of his own best friend, he wrote,

> In the friendship I speak of, our souls mingle and blend with each other so completely that they efface the seam that joined them, and cannot find it again. If you press me to tell why I loved him, I feel that this cannot be expressed, except by answering: Because it was he, because it was I.
>
> Beyond all my understanding, beyond what I can say about this in particular, there was I know not what inexplicable and fateful force that was the mediator of this union. . . . Our friendship has no other model than itself, and can be compared only with itself. (From "On Friendship," by Michel de Montaigne, 1588/1993, p. 139)

Montaigne's conception of love is very poetic, but it is also problematic. By saying that true love transcends reason, he leaves himself without a basis for justifying his love. This makes his love seem whimsical. Is Montaigne's love so free that he can change his mind in the blink of an eye? If you loved someone yesterday for no reason at all, then what is there to keep you from loving someone else today, and yet another person tomorrow? Reasons seem to be the only thing to keep love from becoming fickle. Fickleness could easily destroy a romance or a friendship.

As Jen points out in the dialogue at the beginning of this chapter, there are many different kinds of love. In his book, *The Four Loves* (1960), the British philosopher and novelist C. S. Lewis (1898–1963) identified four main categories of love: romance, friendship, family love, and religious love. He noted that close friendship is an extremely important aspect of life that is underappreciated in our culture. It is not celebrated in music and movies nearly as often as is romantic love. Why do you suppose that is?

In this chapter, we have seen that love is the human response to beauty. Montaigne challenged Plato's view about the rationality of love, but he did not challenge Plato's view about the existence of beauty itself. You can learn more about Plato in Appendix B at the end of this book.

Thought Experiment: The Replacement Brother

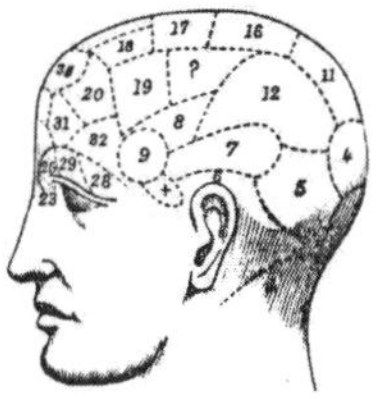

Suppose you have a brother named Jimmy whom you love very much. One day, a crazy magician kills Jimmy, but then instantly replaces him with an exact copy. This copy is the same as Jimmy in every way, including implanted memories of the past. Would you still cry over Jimmy's death? According to Plato, you need not, because the copy reflects the Form of Beauty in the same way. Would you accept the substitute and love it just as you loved the original? According to Plato, you should love them equally well. Many find this answer strange and therefore reject Plato's theory.

Discussion Questions

1. Review the dialogue at the beginning of this chapter. Would Jen agree more with Plato or Montaigne? What about Matt? Give evidence.
2. Construct a real-life example of having to choose between two people (e.g., an old friend versus a new romantic interest). Is the choice rational or irrational in your view? How would you defend yourself if someone thought differently from you?
3. Do you agree with Plato that the Form of Beauty is reflected in all beautiful things? Why or why not?
4. Which is more important to you: being rational or being free? Explain why.
5. Do you think it is possible for a friendship love to change into a romantic love? Do you think the reverse is possible? Do you think it is possible to have both with the same person at the same time?

Exercises

1. Write a dialogue between Janelle and C. S. Lewis. Janelle argues that there are other kinds of love that Lewis left out, for example, love of an object, such as your favorite pair of shoes, or love of an abstract idea, such as democracy. Lewis denies that these are separate categories of love.
2. Construct a thought experiment to test the claim that true love is irrational.

Activities

1. Write some lyrics for a song that expresses your own philosophy of love.
2. Write a letter to your best friend, telling him or her why you love him or her. (You don't have to send it. But, why wouldn't you?)

3. Watch the movie *Romeo and Juliet* (1968), directed by Franco Zeffirelli. Can you identify four relationships in the movie representing C. S. Lewis's four categories of love?

Community Action Steps

1. Go with a group to an outward-bound obstacle course to build friendships.
2. Read a novel to an elderly relative to show you care.
3. Become a Big Brother or a Big Sister for a local youth.
4. Volunteer at a teen crisis hotline.
5. Plan a Valentine's Day celebration at your school.

References

de Montaigne, M. (1993). On friendship. In D. Frame (Trans. & Ed.), *The complete essays* (pp. 135–145). Stanford, CA: Stanford University Press. (Original work written 1572–1576)

Homer (n.d.). *The odyssey*. Retrieved November 28, 2005, from http://classics.mit.edu/Homer/odyssey.html (Original work written 800 BC)

Lewis, C. S. (1960). *The four loves*. New York: Harcourt, Brace.

Plato (n.d.). *Symposium*. Retrieved November 28, 2005, from http://classics.mit.edu/Plato/symposium.html (Original work written 360 BC)

Further Reading

Cere, D. (2001, Spring). Courtship today. *Public Interest, 143*, 53–72.

Friedman, M. (1993). *What are friends for? Feminist perspectives on personal relationships and moral theory*. Ithaca, NY: Cornell University Press.

de Montaigne, M. (1993). On friendship. In D. Frame (Trans. & Ed.), *The complete essays* (pp. 135–145). Stanford, CA: Stanford University Press. (Original work written 1572–1576)

Homer (n.d.). *The odyssey.* Retrieved November 28, 2005, from http://classics.mit.edu/Homer/odyssey.html (Original work written 800 BC)

Lamb, R. E. (Ed.). (1997). *Love analyzed.* Boulder, CO: Westview.

Lewis, C. S. (1960). *The four loves.* New York: Harcourt, Brace.

Nussbaum, M. (1990). *Love's knowledge: Essays on philosophy and literature.* New York: Oxford University Press.

Pakaluk, M. (Ed.). (1991). *Other selves: Philosophers on friendship.* Indianapolis, IN: Hackett.

Plato (n.d.). *Symposium.* Retrieved November 28, 2005, from http://classics.mit.edu/Plato/symposium.html (Original work written 360 BC)

Rouner, L. (Ed.). (1994). *The changing face of friendship.* Notre Dame, IN: University of Notre Dame Press.

Velásquez, E. A. (Ed.). (2003). *Love and friendship: Rethinking politics and affection in modern times.* Lanham, MD: Lexington Books.

Wadell, P. J. (1989). *Friendship and the moral life.* Notre Dame, IN: University of Notre Dame Press.

CHAPTER 2

Is Beauty a Matter of Fact or a Matter of Taste?

The Tackle

Duana and Zach are watching a football game on television. Suddenly, Duana jumps up and shouts, knocking into a bowl of popcorn and spilling it everywhere.

DUANA: <*Still staring at the screen*> Did you see that? What a beautiful tackle! <*She turns to Zach to see why Zach is not responding.*>

ZACH: <*Looking annoyed*> You don't know what you're talking about, hon. <He gets up and brushes popcorn off his shirt.>

DUANA: <*Shocked*> Sure I do.

ZACH: Well, I used to be a football coach, and I'm telling you, that tackle was ugly. The linemen were all over the place, and they almost fell out of bounds.

DUANA: I don't care if you're the King of France, Zach, you can't tell me what to call beautiful. Beauty is whatever anybody wants it to be.

ZACH: <*Zach shakes his head in disbelief. He gestures toward an empty pizza box.*> You're telling me that this dirty old thing could be beautiful to somebody?

DUANA: Absolutely.

ZACH: That's crazy. I mean, someone might *say* a dirty old pizza box is beautiful, but that would just show that he or she has bad taste. Some people have good taste and some people don't. Beauty is what people with good taste like.

DUANA: <*She thinks about what Zach said for a minute.*> OK, so how do you know I don't have good taste?

ZACH: Because you called that ugly tackle beautiful!

DUANA: Man, you're just gonna say that anyone you happen to disagree with has bad taste. Why can't we just agree to disagree?

ZACH: Duana, it's like $2 + 2 = 4$. There is no room for disagreement!

DUANA: <*Putting her feet up on the couch in Zach's place*> I say there's no room for dictators like *you*. <*She looks back at the television for a moment and scowls. Then she looks back at Zach and grins.*>

Questions:

- What is Duana's definition of beauty? What is Zach's definition of beauty? With which definition do you agree more, and why?
- Do you think a football tackle can be beautiful? Why or why not? What about a gymnastic performance? What about a dance performance?
- Describe an example of something beautiful. Suppose someone said he did not think it was beautiful. Would that person be wrong, or just have different taste? How would you explain to him why you think it is beautiful?

A Matter of Fact Versus a Matter of Taste

Former President George H. W. Bush is reported to have said that broccoli is bad. Was he right?

Well, perhaps that's the wrong question to ask. The question implies that it is a matter of fact whether or not broccoli is bad. When President Bush said he thought broccoli was bad, all he meant was, "I don't like broccoli."

So, President Bush's claim is not a matter of fact, but a matter of taste. There would be no point in arguing about his claim, because it can be true for him and not true for you. If you like broccoli, you might pity President Bush for missing out on a yummy vegetable, but you could not accuse him of being wrong.

Consider the other end of the spectrum though. Suppose a scientist claims broccoli contains vitamin A. Here we have a factual claim that is true for everyone. It can be proven scientifically. It would seem silly to say to the scientist, "That may be true for you, but it is not true for me."

Our question is: Are statements about beauty matters of fact or matters of taste?

The ancient Greek philosopher Socrates (469–399 BC) holds that statements about beauty are matters of fact. This view is known as *objectivism.* Socrates' most famous follower, Plato, wrote a dialogue called *The Republic* that records Socrates' views. According to Socrates, if a statue is beautiful, then someone who does not like it does not merely have different taste, they are actually wrong. They are failing to acknowledge an artistic fact, just as someone who does not agree that broccoli contains vitamin A is failing to acknowledge a scientific fact.

Although objectivism may seem strange at first, further consideration reveals that people often talk as though it is true. For example, we learn about the "great" artists in school. This implies that it is a fact that their artwork is beautiful. Furthermore, schools regularly award scholarships for artistic talent and hold art contests. Would this make any sense if there were no objective way to judge the quality of the artwork? And, when you tell a friend that a particular musician or sports star is so much better than others, don't you feel as if you are making a factual claim rather than just reporting your personal reaction? If so, maybe Socrates is on to something.

Socrates (469–399 BC) never wrote any books of his own, but he liked to gather with young people in public places to talk about philosophy. Although Socrates is celebrated as a hero now, during his lifetime he was regarded as a criminal, because the authorities thought he was corrupting the minds of young people and teaching them dangerous things. Socrates was arrested and executed for refusing to stop talking about philosophy in public. Perhaps because his enemies realized that they would be creating a martyred hero, Socrates could have escaped, but he decided it would be better to take a stand and die for a good cause. Plato detailed his reasons for this in the dialogue *Crito*. Throughout history, philosophers have often been persecuted and feared this way. Why do you suppose that is?

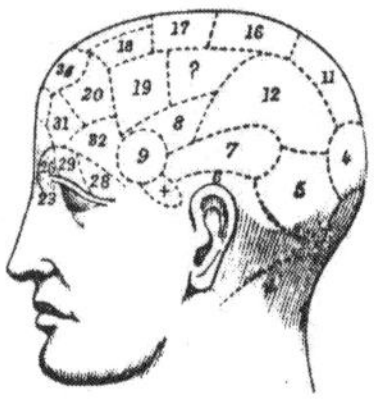

Thought Experiment: Seeing Beauty

Imagine you're on a tour of an art museum. The guide stops your group in front of a painting. "Isn't it beautiful?" she asks. You look at your friend Alec and shrug your shoulders. He says, "Whatever." The guide is determined to get you to agree with her, so she says, "See how bright the colors are." Alec responds, "I see the colors, but I don't see the beauty." The guide grows frustrated: "But, see how energetic the lines are." Alec responds, "I see the lines, but where is the beauty?" The guide has one last try: "Look at how the composition is balanced." Your friend says, "OK, I see balance, but I still don't see any beauty." Would there be any way to convince him?

On the other hand, objectivism leaves us wondering where our idea of beauty originates. How do we know whether a great work of art is beautiful or not? If one person says it is and another says it is not, how will we ever settle the dispute? Socrates' answer is that human beings are born with natural knowledge of beauty. If we all look deep enough, we will come to see the truth. So, someone who disagrees just needs to try harder, just like someone who thinks 2 + 2 = 5 needs to try harder.

The Scottish philosopher David Hume (1711–1776) disagreed with objectivism. In his view, human beings are born without any knowledge at all. Instead, each and every idea about the world that we have in our minds comes from experience. By experience, Hume meant the information we take in through our five senses.

According to Hume, statements about beauty must be a matter of opinion. You never see or hear or taste or touch or smell beauty. There is no way to acquire facts about beauty.

The fact that people disagree about beauty suggests that beauty is not an objective part of the world. Instead, when we judge that something is beautiful, we are announcing our own personal reaction to that thing. Not everyone will react the same way. This view is known as *subjectivism.* A subjectivist holds that the statement "This work of art is beautiful" is a matter of taste, like "I don't like broccoli," rather than a matter of fact, like "Broccoli contains vitamin A."

In defense of the subjectivist view, Hume wrote:

> Thus the distinct boundaries and offices of reason and of taste are easily ascertained. The former conveys the knowledge of truth and falsehood: The latter gives the sentiment of beauty and deformity, vice and virtue. The one discovers objects, as they really stand in nature, without addition or diminution: The other has a productive faculty, and gilding or staining all natural objects with the colours, borrowed from internal sentiment, raises, in a manner, a new

creation. (From *An Enquiry Concerning the Principles of Morals*, by David Hume, 1751/1966, p. 135)

Hume's view is appealing because it means we do not have to search for any final answers about beauty. But, how far does subjectivism go? For Hume, saying that a work of art is terrible means nothing more than saying, "I don't like it." Can the same be said about morality? If you say, "Murder is terrible," does that mean nothing more than saying "I don't like murder"? This is a strange result, because it suggests that it would be perfectly fine for someone to disagree. Yet, it will be hard for Hume to avoid this result because we cannot see or hear or taste or touch or smell morality any more than beauty. Following Hume, someone might go so far as to say everything is subjective. As Shakespeare writes, "There is nothing either good or bad, but thinking makes it so" (from *Hamlet*, Act II, Scene 2). You can learn more about David Hume in Appendix C at the end of the book.

Perhaps subjectivists go too far in saying that everything is a matter of personal taste. In fact, when you look around at how people actually behave, you might be surprised to see just how much agreement there is between people. Notice that even in a disagreement people construct arguments for their positions, indicating that there is a right answer, even if we are not yet certain what it is.

In this chapter we have seen that matters of fact are objective, meaning that they can be right or wrong, while matters of taste are subjective, meaning that they are neither right nor wrong. An opinion could turn out to be a matter of fact or a matter of taste. Opinions are controversial. That's why philosophers love to discuss them.

David Hume (1711–1776) was a Scottish historian and philosopher who lived during a period now known as the Scottish Enlightenment. During this period, Edinburgh, the capital of Scotland was known as the intellectual center of Europe. There were many "societies" formed to discuss ideas, and there Hume would have met, for example, Adam Smith, the founder of modern economic theory. Hume was known for his love of fine company, fine food, and fine drink. But, critics said that his ideas would lead to atheism and immorality, and for more than a century after his death his ideas were largely ignored, until they had quite a spectacular revival in the 20th century. Hume did admit that his view of human reason was rather grim, but he claimed to be able to leave that view in his study and continue to enjoy life.

Discussion Questions

1. Review the dialogue at the beginning of this chapter. Would Duana agree more with Socrates or Hume? What about Zach? Give evidence.
2. Do you think statements about beauty are objective or subjective? Defend your answer.
3. Do you agree with Socrates that human beings are born with natural knowledge of beauty? Why or why not?

4. Do you agree with Hume's belief that all knowledge comes from experience? Why or why not?
5. Socrates is famous for having said "The unexamined life is not worth living." What do you think he meant in this statement?

Exercises

1. Write a dialogue between Tom and Jerry. Tom argues that all values are subjective, and Jerry argues that some are objective.
2. Construct a thought experiment to test the claim that art contests require objective standards.

Activities

1. Draw a picture that demonstrates your conception of beauty.
2. Watch the movie *Pollock* (2000), directed by Ed Harris. Do you think the artwork depicted in this movie is beautiful? Why or why not?
3. Write a report concerning a nearby landmark that you find beautiful.

Community Action Steps

1. Organize a craft workshop for children in your neighborhood.
2. Beautify your school by picking up litter or painting a mural.
3. Visit a school for the blind to discuss nonvisual conceptions of beauty.
4. Interview some older relatives about their tastes in food and then cook a meal for them.

References

Hume, D. (1966). *An enquiry concerning the principles of morals.* Peru, IL: Open Court. (Original work published 1751)

Hume, D. (1993). *An enquiry concerning human understanding.* Indianapolis, IN: Hackett. (Original work published 1772)

Plato (n.d.). *Republic.* Retrieved November 28, 2005, from http://classics.mit.edu/Plato/republic.html (Original work written 360 BC)

Shakespeare, W. (1604). *Hamlet (Folger Shakespeare library).* New York: Washington Square Press. (Original work published 1600–1602)

Further Reading

Berger, J. (1972). *Ways of seeing.* New York: Viking Press.

Bruce, N. (1996, Winter). The immortal David Hume, 1711–1776. *Free Inquiry, 17*(1), 38–40.

Fenton, J. (1997, July 18). What is ideal beauty? *New Statesman, 126,* 44.

Greenberg, C. (1999). *Homemade esthetics: Observations on art and taste.* New York: Oxford University Press.

Hume, D. (1966). *An enquiry concerning the principles of morals.* Peru, IL: Open Court. (Original work published 1751)

Hume, D. (1993). *An enquiry concerning human understanding.* Indianapolis, IN: Hackett. (Original work published 1772)

Kaufman, D. A. (2002, March). Normative criticism and the objective value of artworks. *Journal of Aesthetics & Art Criticism, 60,*151–167.

Lane, M. (2002, January). Was Socrates a democrat? *History Today, 52*(1), 42–47.

Phillips, C. (2001). *Socrates café: A fresh taste of philosophy.* New York: W. W. Norton & Company.

Plato (n.d.). *Republic.* Retrieved November 28, 2005, from http://classics.mit.edu/Plato/republic.html (Original work written 360 BC)

CHAPTER 3
What Is the Purpose of Art?

The Driftwood

Terry goes walking along the lakeshore one day and finds a twisted piece of wood that has drifted up onto the sand. It has an interesting shape and is baked hard by the sun. He brings it home, cleans it off, rubs some oil on it, and sets it in the middle of a table. Then, Terry's brother Lander comes home.

LANDER: <*He gives the driftwood on the table a funny look.*> What's that old piece of junk doing on the table?

TERRY: <*Offended*> It's not junk, it's art.

LANDER: <*Surprised*> That's not art. Art is something you make. <*He picks up the driftwood.*> You didn't make this.

TERRY: I didn't make the wood, but by polishing it, setting it on the table, and giving it a title, I've expressed myself.

LANDER: What's the title?

TERRY: "Troubled Soul."

LANDER: Huh? I don't really get what you're trying to express. Unless you're just trying to say: Look at this ugly piece of wood! <*He chuckles.*>

TERRY: <*Snarling*> It doesn't matter whether you get it or whether you like it. <*He puts his hands to his hips.*> The important thing is that I expressed myself. That's what art is: A way of expressing yourself.

LANDER: If that driftwood was mine, I'd make it into a cat. <*He points to various parts of the driftwood as he continues.*> See how this branch here looks like a long tail, and these branches here look like legs? You could add a Styrofoam head here, and paint it black. Then you could put it in the window on Halloween! <*Lander is really getting interested now, but he soon notices that Terry looks bored.*>

LANDER: Well, at least then people would know what it's supposed to be. It would look like a real black cat.

TERRY: Sure, but who cares! <*Terry throws up his hands.*> There are plenty of real black cats already out there in the world. As an artist, I want to create something completely new out of my own head, not just imitate stuff that already exists.

LANDER: <*Lander looks at the wood again.*> Go for it. <*He shrugs and then continues on his way.*>

Questions

- What is Lander's definition of art? What is Terry's definition of art? With which definition do you agree more, and why?
- Do you think Terry's driftwood is art? Why or why not?
- Describe an example of your own art. Suppose someone said he didn't think it was art. How would you explain to him why you think it is?

The Purpose of Art

Stop for a moment and picture your favorite piece of artwork. Why do you like it? Does it represent something concrete that exists in the world, or does it express an abstract idea? Now, consider your favorite song. Is it happy or sad? Some people prefer upbeat music because they want it to make them feel cheery. Others think cheeriness is superficial. They prefer music that brings out deep emotions, even if this involves fear or pain. Paintings and music are just two of the many different artistic forms, but they demonstrate why philosophers disagree over the purpose of art.

Aristotle (384–322 BC) was an ancient Greek philosopher who promotes the representationalist view of the purpose of art. According to representationalism, art should imitate nature. Although he was not an artist himself, Aristotle wrote about art in his work, *Poetics*. Just as a painting can represent physical objects in the world, music can represent real sounds, for example, a birdsong, rain falling, or thunder crashing. According to Aristotle, human beings enjoy artwork because it reminds us of the beauty of nature.

Friedrich Nietzsche (1844–1900) was a German philosopher who criticized Aristotle's representationalist theory. Nietzsche believed representing the physical world is a shallow form of amusement. He argued instead that the purpose of art is *metaphysical*, meaning that it transcends reality (metaphysics literally means "beyond science"). In his book, *The Birth of Tragedy*, he focused on myth as an art form. Myths have a great deal of artistic value, and yet they are not meant to imitate reality. In fact, they often involve supernatural beings with magical powers. Nor are they always cheerful. Nietzsche was particularly interested in tragic myths that involved death and destruction. Tragic stories have been popular in many cultures throughout history. We might well pause to ask: Why do people want to hear about such terrible things?

Nietzsche's theory is that experiencing unhappiness is actually good for human beings. It forces us to have courage and strive toward greater accomplishments. He wrote:

> The genesis of tragedy cannot be explained by saying that things happen, after all, just as tragically in real life. Art is not an imitation of nature but its metaphysical supplement, raised up beside it in order to overcome it. Insofar

Aristotle (384–322 BC) was the star student at Plato's Academy. He and Plato were great friends even though they disagreed about many things. The Renaissance painter Raphael did a painting called *School of Athens* featuring Plato and Aristotle (a part of it is on the cover of this book). In the picture, Raphael portrays Plato pointing up toward the sky and Aristotle pointing down toward the ground. This is meant to symbolize their disagreement. Plato, as we have seen, was interested in abstract ideas that transcend this world, while Aristotle was interested more in concrete physical objects. Many of his books were the first to bear, as titles, many of the sciences we know today. Aristotle later started his own school called The Lyceum, where among other things he collected samples of plants and animals to study.

as tragic myth belongs to art, it fully shares its transcendent intentions. . . . For now we can really grasp the significance of the need to look and yet go beyond that look. The auditory analogue of this experience is musical dissonance, as used by a master, which makes us need to hear and at the same time to go beyond that hearing. (From *The Birth of Tragedy*, by Friedrich Nietzsche, 1871/1956, pp. 142–143)

In another work, *Twilight of the Idols,* Nietzsche wrote, "If you have your *why* of life then you can get along with almost any *how.* Man does *not* strive for happiness; only the English do that" (1888/1998, Aphorism 12, p. 6). In Nietzsche's view, it is better to be sad and deep than to be happy and superficial. One of his most famous sayings can be paraphrased as "whatever doesn't kill you will make you stronger."

There are problems, however, with the idea that suffering is beneficial. Should we deliberately hurt ourselves in order to overcome the pain? Should we deliberately hurt others? Nietzsche suggested that, rather than being angry with the muggers who knock you down and steal your wallet, you should thank them for making you stronger!

Every culture around the world has its own unique myths that help to shape the identity of the people. Consider the creation myth of the Yoruba tribe in Nigeria. According to it, before being born into the physical world, every human must visit the workshop of the heavenly potter Ajalamopin to choose one of several premade "inner heads." The inner head is something like a soul that you cannot physically see. Each inner head contains a different type of power. The head you choose determines the power you have, which in turn determines your fate in the physical world. This metaphysical perspective affects the way the Yoruba see themselves. If you choose the wrong inner head, you may be destined to live a very unlucky life. The Yoruba have many stories about the problems people run into due to the choice they made before they were born.

Despite their considerable disagreement, one thing both Aristotle and Nietzsche have in common is the view that artists should be concerned with how their works will affect the audience. In their view, artists should create for the sake of those who will appreciate the creation. The philosophy of art known as *expressionism* denies this. It holds that the purpose of art is to express the artist's innermost thoughts and feelings. In creating a work of art, the artist should not be concerned about what others think of it.

Expressionism also lends itself to political activism. In the 20th century, more and more people began to use art to make a statement. For example, the late Tupac Shakur, one of the most famous American rap artists, made strong statements about inner-city life. His work is controversial because it uses explicit language that many find offensive.

To an expressionist, it does not matter how the audience reacts. Furthermore, because the U.S. Constitution protects freedom of speech, no one can prevent artists from expressing many things that offend other people.

There are, however, some problems with this philosophy. Many people are worried that explicit language, violence, and sex are harmful to children. They argue that we have a moral obligation to protect children from words and images that they are too young to understand. Others go so far as to say that today's artistic statements are escalating beyond what's healthy even for adults. Each new artist goes a little further than the last. Where will it stop? Art was once considered to be the mark of advanced civilizations. If our art becomes corrosive of moral values, some people argue, it may become the downfall of our civilization.

In this chapter, we have surveyed three different theories concerning the purpose of art. Each has its pros and cons showing that art is related in a complicated way to beauty and to the way we see ourselves.

Suppose Aristotle is correct in his belief that the purpose of art is to represent reality. This does not necessarily imply that paintings should always be photographically accurate or that music should sound like a tape recording of things happening in the world. Consider the work of the French Impressionists, such as Claude Monet. Monet's paintings are always blurry and vague. He paints this way deliberately, because he wants to capture the way sunlight makes things shimmer. Because sunlight is part of nature, and his paintings are intended to represent light, they are still representational works. Aristotle would approve.

Palazzo da Mula, Venice, 1908, Claude Monet

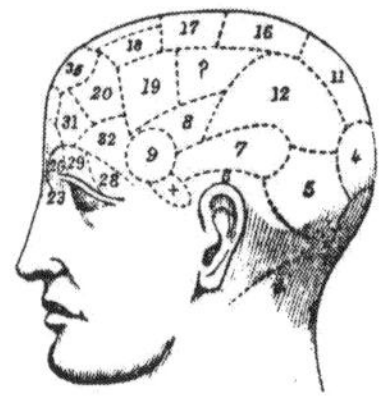

Thought Experiment: The Nature of Art

Suppose you find a beautiful rock formation while out in the woods. Experts study it and declare that it is a statue made by a primitive and now extinct group of people. So, you donate it to an art museum, where it sits for many years and is admired by many people. Then, new evidence is uncovered that shows that it is a natural rock formation, made by rain dripping from a cave wall. Can the rock formation still be art? Should it be moved from the Museum of Art to the Museum of Natural History? What do you think you will say when you look at it again? Do you think it will look any different to you than it did when you first saw it?

Discussion Questions

1. Review the dialogue at the beginning of this chapter. Is Terry a representationalist or an expressionist? What about Lander? Give evidence.
2. As we have seen, Aristotle thought art should represent reality, and Nietzsche thought art should be tragic. What do you think they would think about Tupac's raps? Why?
3. Have you ever been offended by someone's artwork? If so, describe it. If not, imagine some artwork you might find offensive.
4. Which do you value more: being happy and lighthearted or thinking about deep and difficult things? Explain why.
5. Do you think it is possible for a work of art to represent reality and transcend reality at the same time? If not, why? If so, give an example.
6. Suppose a friend shows you a photograph that you really like. You congratulate your friend. But, then you learn that a computer program has enhanced it. Will you think less of your friend as a photographer?

Exercises

1. Write a dialogue between Mark and Tierra. Mark argues that explicit language in music should be censored. Tierra argues that it shouldn't.
2. Construct a thought experiment to test the claim that suffering makes you strong.

Activities

1. Make a drawing that demonstrates your own philosophy of art.
2. Write a tragic myth for modern times.
3. Visit an art museum. Arrange for a guided tour.
4. Watch the movie *Surviving Picasso* (1996), directed by James Ivory. Was Picasso a representationalist or an expressionist in your view?

Community Action Steps

1. Go with a group to a political art exhibit or concert in your area.
2. Play music or do crafts at a nursing home.
3. Put on a play at your school that dramatizes an issue you are concerned about.
4. Invite a controversial artist to your school.
5. Organize an art fair where people in your neighborhood can show their work.

References

Aristotle (n.d.). *Poetics*. Retrieved November 28, 2005, from http://classics.mit.edu/Aristotle/poetics.html (Original work written 350 BC)

Nietzsche, F. (1956). *The birth of tragedy* (F. Golffing, Trans.). Garden City, NY: Doubleday. (Original work published 1871)

Nietzsche, F. (1998). *Twilight of the idols* (D. Large, Trans.). New York: Oxford University Press. (Original work published 1888)

Further Reading

Aristotle (n.d.). *Poetics.* Retrieved November 28, 2005, from http://classics.mit.edu/Aristotle/poetics.html (Original work written 350 BC)

Carroll, N. E. (1998). *A philosophy of mass art.* Oxford, England: Oxford University Press.

Bayles, M. (1998, Spring). Body and soul: The musical miseducation of the youth. *Public Interest, 131,* 36–49,

Danto, A. C. (1993). After the end of art. *Artforum International, 31*(8), 62–69.

Freeland, C. (2003). *Art theory: A very short introduction.* Oxford, England: Oxford University Press.

Lamarque, P., & Olsen, S. H. (Eds.). (2004). *Aesthetics and the philosophy of art: The analytic tradition.* Oxford, England: Blackwell.

Nietzsche, F. (1956). *The birth of tragedy* (F. Golffing, Trans.). Garden City, NY: Doubleday. (Original work published 1871)

Nietzsche, F. (1998). *Twilight of the idols* (D. Large, Trans.). New York: Oxford University Press. (Original work published 1888)

Sheppard, A. (1987). *Aesthetics: An introduction to the philosophy of art.* Oxford, England: Oxford University Press.

Warburton, N. (2003). *The art question.* New York: Routledge.

CHAPTER 4
Is There a Difference Between Health and Beauty?

The Babies

Ashley and Elizabeth are volunteers in the neonatal unit of a local hospital. They both want to become doctors. Many of the new babies in the unit have serious diseases, and Ashley and Elizabeth are supposed to feed and comfort them. They are waiting for the elevator.

ASHLEY: Working here just breaks my heart. Even most of the kids who survive will be scarred for life, or crippled, or not have all their marbles. Sometimes I think it would be better if they were never born at all.

ELIZABETH: Don't say that! It's better to be alive, even if you're not perfect.

ASHLEY: I'm not so sure about that, Elizabeth. Dr. Brown says many of these diseases can be identified during pregnancy. I think if a pregnant woman knows her fetus is abnormal, she should terminate the pregnancy and try again.

ELIZABETH: <*Elizabeth raises her eyebrows.*> You mean have an abortion? I'm against abortion. I think human life is a sacred gift from God.

ASHLEY: I don't. I think human life is a product of the survival of the fittest. We evolved from simple life forms over millions of years and those that aren't fit—

ELIZABETH: <*Elizabeth interjects.*> Oh, come on! Everyone needs a little help to survive. Anyway, genetic engineering will soon make it possible for us to avoid diseases in the first place. Just think: Before long people will be able to have whatever type of baby they want by selecting genes from a test tube.

ASHLEY: I don't like the idea of engineering human genes. <*She thinks about it for a moment.*> It seems to me like playing God.

ELIZABETH: Don't be silly, Ashley. If you were pregnant and the doctor told you to take vitamins would you?

ASHLEY: Of course—to have a healthy baby.

ELIZABETH: Well, selecting genes from a test tube is just a more efficient way of having a healthy baby.

ASHLEY: <*Ashley looks doubtful.*> But, where will it end? The next thing you know people will be designing babies to be taller or smarter. We'll create an army of Barbie dolls that all look and think alike.

<*Elizabeth shakes her head emphatically while Ashley nods.*>

Questions

- What is Elizabeth's definition of human life? What is Ashley's definition? With whom do you agree more, and why?
- Do you think that if people could "design" their children, most would choose to enhance the same features? What features would you choose and why?
- Do you think people with a high risk of passing on serious diseases should or should not have children? What about less serious problems like acne and crooked teeth?
- Do you think we value appearance too much in our society?

Health and Beauty

In our society we value physical appearance, often more than personality. Notice how we care more about what celebrities are wearing than about what they have to say. Consider how much time women spend trying to get skinny, and how much time men spend trying to buff up. Is this obsession with appearance healthy? Does the current availability and use of various cosmetic enhancements endanger our dignity?

Your body is constructed according to your genetic blueprint. Your father gave you half of your genes and your mother gave you the other half. But, which of your father and mother's genes you receive and how they will combine is a matter of luck. The genetic "lottery" determines what physical traits you inherit, including your risk for particular diseases. What will happen when we can engineer this process so that we do not have to rely on luck any more?

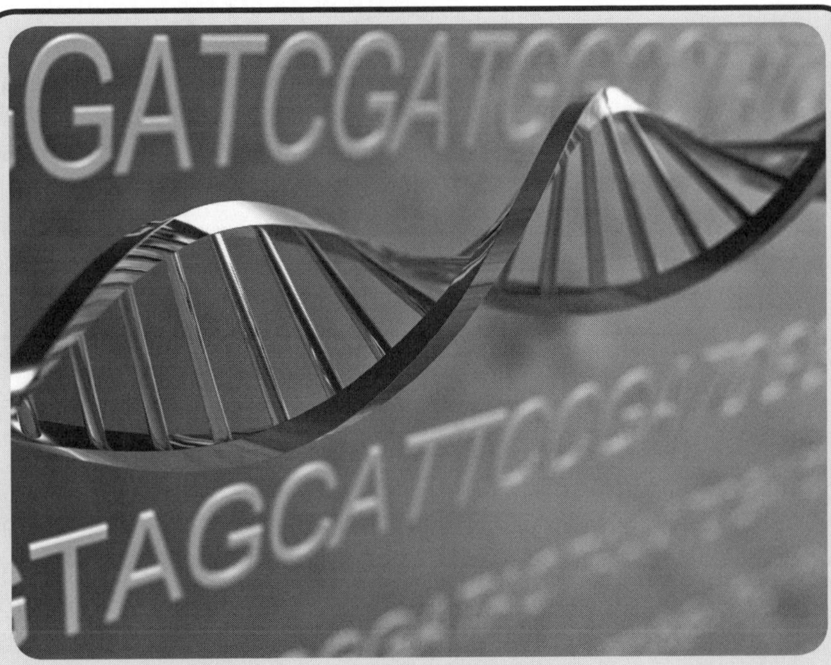

Genetic engineering is a new science that studies the microscopic structure of living tissue. In the late 20th century, genetic engineers began the Human Genome Project, which has now successfully mapped the entire human genetic code. This information is already being used to treat human beings, either by eliminating problem genes or by adding desirable genes. Genetic treatment is controversial because it enables us to make choices about our bodies that were previously determined naturally.

Of course, the genetic makeup of a child has never been completely unplanned or unpredictable, because human beings choose their mates in part on the basis of physical condition and appearance. The advent of new reproductive technologies, however, has increased that control. Even now, it is common to find ads in college newspapers soliciting donors for egg and sperm banks. People who buy eggs and sperm from these banks often specify what sorts of physical traits they are looking for in a donor. Or, they request donors of a certain occupation in the hope of having children with certain physical or mental aptitudes. On the Internet, there are ads soliciting human eggs, often for very high payments, which stipulate height, body type, skin color, minimum SAT scores, and the like. A process called *in vitro fertilization* is currently used by many people who want to have a child, but have problems with fertility. With this process, eggs and sperm are united in a lab and allowed to grow for a while in a Petri dish before being implanted in a woman's womb. Increasingly, we are able to perform genetic screening on these embryos. So, genetic engineering has the potential, both promising and frightening, to revolutionize how we think about human beings. This knowledge will soon allow us to select the genetic makeup of our children. We may direct the next stage in human evolution.

Most people welcome this new scientific knowledge when it can be used to cure serious diseases, but many are disturbed at the thought of allowing parents to choose what kind of children they want. As we saw in the dialogue at the beginning of this chapter, Ashley argues that we should not "play God," and that if we do use genetic engineering, we will end up with a nation of perfect replicas. Are these concerns justified?

A good response to the concern about playing God is to point out that we already do it. When we give medical treatment, we are playing God. Some people say genetic treatment is unnatural. But, so are a lot of common procedures. If your kidneys fail and you have to use an artificial kidney machine, that is not natural. To be sure, there are religious sects that refuse any modern medicine, but if a child in one of these sects is critically ill, the government almost always orders that the child be treated. There is nothing unusual about genetic engineering when it is used to treat diseases. In fact, it is liable to be easier and more effective than other treatments.

Leon Kass, a bioethicist and the science ethics adviser to President George W. Bush, is critical of genetic engineering. He argues that performing genetic screening tests on unborn children and aborting those that do not measure up, or selecting genes for your child from a test tube, will inevitably lead to an increase in discrimination. The reason is that there will always be people who choose not to practice any kind of genetic engineering, or who cannot afford to do so. This means that a group of individuals that some might consider to be less than perfect will still exist. They will grow up knowing that a large segment of the population regards them as inferior or defective.

W. French Anderson (1936–), an early genetic researcher, has a different concern about genetic engineering. He argues that we run the risk of making mistakes with widespread consequences. For example, if we allow parents to select particular characteristics, and they all tend to select the same ones, then we will eventually lose diversity in our society. If the old saying that "variety is the spice of life" is true, then we may one day wish that we had not become so similar. Even more importantly, lack of genetic diversity can be dangerous for a species. Having a wide variety of characteristics is what allows organisms to survive harsh conditions and unexpected diseases. If the members of the human species become too similar, it may become vulnerable to extinction.

Thought Experiment: Just the Way You Are

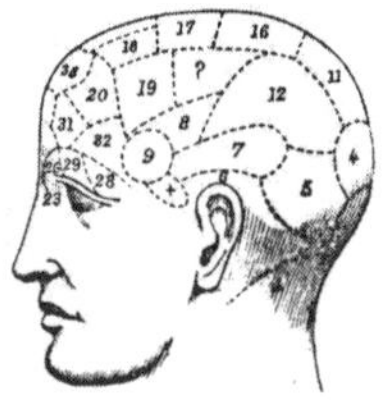

Imagine that it is the year 2050 and it has become popular to select children that are tall and have clear skin. Your parents, however, could not afford genetic selection, and so you are short and have acne. Imagine further that you are the only person in your neighborhood who is short and has acne. How would you feel? When you ask your parents why you are the only person like you on the whole block, they respond that the neighbors had their fetuses tested. If the fetuses had genes that would cause the resulting child to grow up short with acne, they were aborted. Would this make you feel unwanted? Why or why not?

On the other hand, it is not clear that genetic engineering would destroy diversity. After all, right now it's possible to get a nose job, and wealthy people do it all the time, but they don't all choose the same nose. To get an idea of whether genetically engineered children would end up looking and acting the same, conduct a survey of your family and friends. Make a list of 20 physical and behavioral characteristics, and ask which ones they would choose, or what feature they think is most important.

Anderson argues that we should use gene therapy only to treat serious diseases, and never for enhancement. By treating serious diseases, he means correcting debilitating or fatal conditions; by enhancement, he means making changes in appearance or ability. He adds that we should only use gene therapy on body cells and never on reproductive cells. Changes made to reproductive cells will continue to be present in future generations, while changes to body cells die whenever the patient dies. Anderson argues that limiting gene therapy to body cells reduces the possibility that any mistakes that have been made will have long-term consequences.

Some people point out that it is impossible to draw a hard and fast line between serious disease and enhancement. There will always be borderline cases. Poor vision is a good example. Suppose you undergo gene therapy to improve your 20/40 to 20/20 vision. Is that curing a debilitating condition or enhancing ability?

Although Anderson's distinction is admittedly vague, something like it is already in use. Most health care policies have lists of procedures that they will and will not cover. For example, if you want cosmetic surgery, most insurance companies will not pay for the necessary surgery. But, if you need reconstructive surgery because of cancer in a certain body part, the same surgery will be covered. Do you think this is a fair practice? Why or why not?

Clearly, questions about beauty are not just abstract puzzles. In this chapter, we have seen that different concepts of beauty raise serious ethical issues. Thinking about these issues philosophically can help us make good choices about the future consequences of genetic engineering.

Discussion Questions

1. Review the dialogue at the beginning of this chapter. Do you think Elizabeth would accept Anderson's restrictions on genetic engineering? What about Ashley? Give evidence.
2. Are piercing and tattooing ways of making yourself unique or ways of making yourself a replica of everybody else?
3. Do you think people who are obsessed with their appearance are shallow? Why or why not?
4. Would you select your children's genes through genetic engineering? Would you do it only for disease prevention, or for physical enhancements, as well? Why or why not?
5. Do you think genetic engineering is "playing God"? What about conventional treatments, such as kidney transplants—is that playing God, too? Why or why not?

Exercises

1. Write a dialogue between Brent and Caroline, who are both deaf. They have just had a baby boy who is deaf, as well. There is a treatment to correct the baby's deafness. Brent argues that the baby should have the treatment. Caroline argues that he should not so that he can be a part of their deaf community.

2. Construct a thought experiment to test the claim that genetic testing and engineering will inevitably lead to an increase in discrimination.

Activities

1. Write a poem that captures your view of the essence of human dignity.
2. Draw a picture that expresses the pros and cons of diversity.
3. Write a report on the most recent developments in genetic engineering.
4. Watch the movie *Gattaca* (1997), directed by Andrew Niccol. How realistic do you think it is?

Community Action Steps

1. Volunteer in the neonatal unit of a local hospital.
2. Join a pro-life or pro-choice activist organization.
3. Visit a handicapped friend or relative.
4. Write a letter to Leon Kass expressing your view of genetic engineering.

References

Anderson, W. F. (1990). Genetics and human malleability. *The Hastings Center Report, 20*, 21–24.

Kass, L. (1973). Implications of prenatal diagnosis for the human right to life. In B. Hilton et al. (Eds.), *Ethical issues in human genetics: Genetic counseling and the use of genetic knowledge* (pp. 185–199). New York: Plenum Press.

Further Reading

Allchin, D. (2005). Sacred bovines: Genes 'r' us. *American Biology Teacher, 67,* 244–247.

Anderson, W. F. (1990, January/February). Genetics and human malleability. *The Hastings Center Report, 20,* 21–24.

Chapkis, W. (1986). *Beauty secrets: Women and the politics of appearance.* Boston: South End Press.

Galston, W. A. (2002, Fall). What's at stake in biotech? *Public Interest, 149,* 103–108

Kass, L. (1973). Implications of prenatal diagnosis for the human right to life. In B. Hilton et al. (Eds.), *Ethical issues in human genetics: Genetic counseling and the use of genetic knowledge* (pp. 185–199). New York: Plenum Press.

Morgentaler, H. (1996). The moral case for abortion. *Free Inquiry, 16*(3), 17–21.

Peters, T. (1996, October 30). In search of the perfect child: Genetic testing and selective abortion. *The Christian Century, 113,* 1034–1037.

Shannon, T. (Ed.). (2004). *Reproductive technologies: A reader.* Lanham, MD: Rowman & Littlefield.

Simons, J. (2005, May 2). The quest for custom cures. *Fortune, 151,* 107–111.

Somerville, M. A. (2000). *The ethical canary: Science, society and the human spirit.* Toronto, ON, Canada: Viking/Penguin Canada.

PART 2

Truth

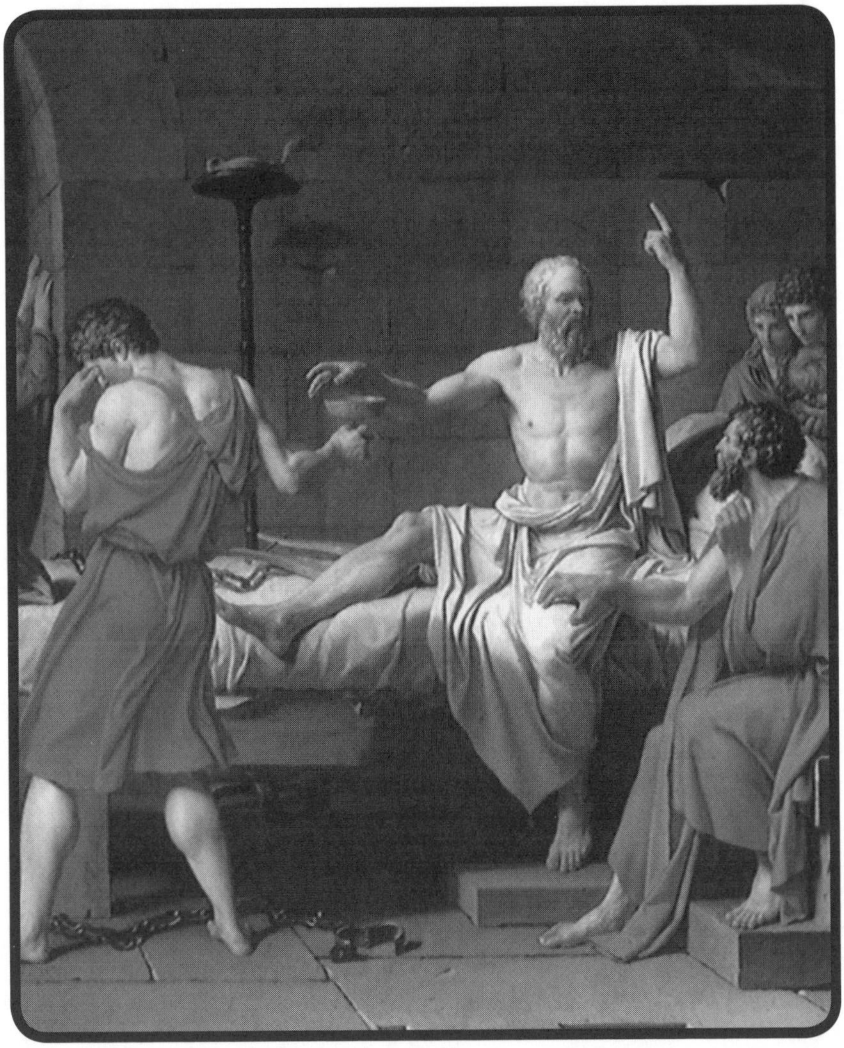

The Death of Socrates, 1787, Jacques-Louis David

CHAPTER 5
Is There Anything That Cannot Be True?

The Dream

Dylan is sitting in the break room at work reading a book. Suddenly the door bursts open and Alexandra comes running in, all out of breath. When she sees Dylan on the couch, she dashes over.

ALEXANDRA: <*Shouting*> Dylan, you have to help me! Can you see me right now?

DYLAN: <*Looking up from his book, annoyed*> Of course I can see you. I can hear you too. Why are you shouting?

ALEXANDRA: Because I'm not sure if you're real. <*She reaches out to touch him.*>

DYLAN: <*Dylan slaps her hand away.*> Are you crazy, girl? What's your problem?

ALEXANDRA: I was just walking to work and a strange old man came up to me in the street. He told me I was dreaming.

DYLAN: And, you believed him?

ALEXANDRA: Not at first. I told him I was wide awake. But, he looked straight into my eyes and said, "Prove it!" That's when I remembered that sometimes I wake up from a dream, but then it turns out that waking up is part of the dream. Has that ever happened to you?

DYLAN: <*Beginning to understand*> Yeah, I guess. So, what did you do?

ALEXANDRA: I pinched myself. I told the old man that I would have woken up if I pinched myself while I was asleep. But, he said I could have just dreamed that I pinched myself!

DYLAN: <*Patting her shoulder*> Well, I can assure you that this is no dream.

ALEXANDRA: But, what if I'm dreaming you, too?

DYLAN: Alexandra, you've known me since we were little kids. You can't dream for that long! Besides, don't you think I would know if I was just your dream?

ALEXANDRA: The memory of our childhood could be part of the dream. Maybe I'm your dream and you're mine.

DYLAN: Let me get this straight. You're saying that in order to find out whether or not you're dreaming you would already have to know whether or not you're dreaming.

ALEXANDRA: Yes, exactly.

DYLAN: But, if you already knew, you wouldn't need to find out!

ALEXANDRA: Now you see why I'm so freaked.

DYLAN: Yeah, I'd say you're pretty much screwed. <*Folding his arms.*>

ALEXANDRA: Jeez! Thanks, Dylan, you've been a huge help.

Questions

- How does Alexandra try to prove she isn't dreaming? How does Dylan try to prove she isn't dreaming? Which argument do you find more convincing, and why?
- Do you think that it is possible that you are dreaming right now? Why or why not?
- Describe an example of a dream you thought was real while you were dreaming it.
- Suppose someone told you that you are dreaming right now. How would you prove them wrong?

Something That Cannot Be True

A *paradox* is a situation that looks normal on the surface, but when you look deeper, you find a contradiction that makes the situation impossible. We can apply this definition to the above dialogue. It seems normal enough that Alexandra wants to find out whether or not she's dreaming. But, upon further consideration, it becomes evident that in order to find out, she would have to know already. The situation seems to imply both that she knows and that she doesn't know. But, this is a contradiction. A *contradiction* occurs when you both assert and deny the very same thing. Contradictions cannot be true because they describe an impossible state of affairs.

The Dutch artist MC Escher is famous for incorporating paradoxes into his artwork. Imagine two hands, each drawing each other. At first glance it seems like a perfectly straightforward idea. But, on second thought, how can the first hand be drawing the second hand if the second hand is drawing the first hand? The first hand would have to exist in order to do the drawing, but if it already existed, then it would not need to be drawn by the second hand. It seems like each hand exists in virtue of drawing and at the same time does not exist in virtue of needing to be drawn. But, to exist and not to exist at the same time is a contradiction. So, the image is a paradox.

Perhaps the most famous paradox in philosophy is called the liar paradox. It goes like this: Suppose Zeppie says, "I'm lying." This looks like an ordinary statement. If it is, then it should be either true or false. The problem is that it cannot be either. Here's why:

1. First, suppose that it is true. If what Zeppie says is true, then she is lying. But, liars tell falsehoods. If Zeppie is a liar, then what she is saying is false. So, if you suppose the statement is true, it turns out to be false.
2. Second, suppose that it is false. If what Zeppie says is false, then she is not lying. But, if she is not lying, then she is telling the truth. If she is telling the truth then she is a liar, because she claims she is not telling the truth. But, this means that her statement is true after all. So, if you suppose the statement is false, it turns out to be true.

Does this make your head spin?

René Descartes (1596–1650) was a French philosopher who challenged his readers to try to prove that they are not dreaming. In a popular book called *Meditations on First Philosophy*, he asks, "How can you be certain your whole life is not a dream?" Descartes went even further to ask, "What if your whole life is a hoax put on by a powerful, but evil genius?" His own answer to the question is that even if your whole life is a hoax, you can know one thing for certain: You do exist. If you did not exist, there would be no one there to hoax. This is to say that, if you think you exist, you must actually exist. Descartes stated his solution in the famous formula, "I think, therefore I am." Descartes was also a brilliant mathematician and scientist who invented the Cartesian coordinate system.

Similar to the liar paradox is the lawyer paradox. It goes like this: Dr. Peters is a professor in a prominent law school. Sarah wants to enroll at this school, but she has no money. So, the following contract is made: Dr. Peters will teach Sarah the law without charging her any tuition. When Sarah finishes her studies, she will pay tuition to Dr. Peters only if she wins her first case. If Sarah loses her first case, her education will have been free.

After finishing her studies, Sarah announces that her first case will be to sue Dr. Peters for free tuition. She argues that no matter how the case turns out, she does not have to pay him. If she wins the suit, she wins free tuition, and if she loses it, then, because it is her first case, her contract with Dr. Peters guarantees her free tuition.

Dr. Peters responds that, on the contrary, if she sues him she will have to pay tuition whether she wins or loses. If she wins her first case, then their contract compels her to pay. If she loses, then she has lost the suit to be awarded free tuition and so the court will compel her to pay.

A judge must decide whether Sarah or Dr. Peters is right. You are that judge. Do you side with Sarah or Dr. Peters? Defend your answer.

Then there is "Zeno's Paradox," illustrated in the following scenario: Alicia is a much better basketball player than Zeno, but Zeno bets Alicia that she will never beat him, and can prove this without ever setting foot on the court. Zeno argues that for Alicia to get to the basket from her end of the court, she first has to get to the center court line. But, to get to the center court line, she has to get halfway there first. And, of course she first has to get halfway to the halfway mark. And, so on and so on forever. Alicia can never get to the other end of the court, Zeno argues, because there are an infinite number of halfway points in between. This is a paradox, because the idea of traveling from point A to point B seems perfectly plausible, until you look at the mathematics of the situation (use the diagram to the left to work out the paradox for yourself).

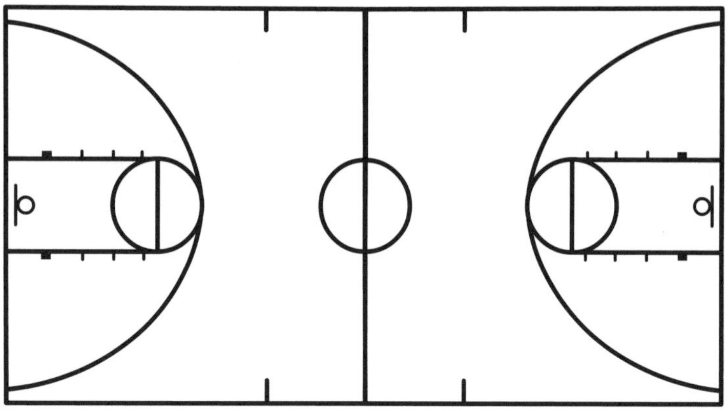

According to some people, the solution to this paradox is to deny that there are an infinite number of halfway points between A and B. Although there may be an infinite number of points on a geometrical line, geometrical lines do not really exist. They are imaginary. The paradox arises from trying to impose our imagination onto the world. Do you think this solution works?

Although paradoxes make fun puzzles, they also have serious significance. Logicians believe paradoxes tell us a great deal about human language and the structure of thought. Furthermore, if you can show that someone's theory is mired in paradox, you have a good refutation of that theory.

The theory of relativism is a good example of a theory mired in paradox. At a superficial level, relativism seems true. But, at a deeper level it involves contradictions and therefore refutes itself.

Relativism is the theory that there is no such thing as a single truth for everyone. Instead, everyone has his or her own set of truths. This view is motivated by the observation that everyone has different values. All you have to do is look around the world and see that people disagree. For example, some people think it is true that God exists; others think it is false. Relativists say that there is no point in saying that one is right and the other is wrong. If you believe in God, then the statement "God exists" is true for you. If you do not believe in God, then it is not true for you.

Relativists are concerned about promoting tolerance of differing points of view. They reason that if everyone is allowed to have their own set of truths, then we will feel no need to win the argument all of the time and put other people down. Wars have been fought over differing value systems. Relativism would put an end to such conflicts because everyone would be welcome to believe what they want.

Most philosophers reject relativism because they believe that the truth is objective and a matter of fact, the same for everyone, even when we do not know what it is. For example, we do not yet know what the cure for AIDS is, but scientists are looking, because we all believe that we will someday find a cure for it. Some philosophers argue against Richard Rorty's beliefs (see the box on the right), saying that, while tolerance and ending violence are noble goals, relativism cannot be the way to reach them. Consider the following relativist statements:

"You should never tell anyone else what to do."
"There are no absolute truths."
"No statement is universally true."

Can you see what is paradoxical about each of these statements?

The American philosopher Richard Rorty (1931–) is a relativist. Although Rorty is a philosopher, he is critical of philosophy because of its emphasis on argument. As Rorty puts it, if you argue against my theory, you are conveying the message that you think you are right and I am wrong. Rorty thinks it is silly to accuse anyone of being wrong on issues where it is impossible to find a definite answer. He thinks that instead we should engage in friendly and cooperative conversation. Most philosophers throughout history have rejected this attitude, because they believe that arguing is a beneficial way of searching for answers. Although relativism is not popular among philosophers, it is often popular among sociologists, whose job it is to compare different cultures without judging them.

The standard view among philosophers is that relativism is self-refuting because it contradicts itself. This does not mean, however, that we should give up on tolerance and peace. One can be tolerant without thinking that truth is relative to each individual. It could be that there is one single truth, but because it is very difficult to know for sure what it is, we must try to be tolerant of differing opinions.

Discussion Questions

1. Explain a paradox you have encountered. Were you able to solve it?
2. How would you solve the liar paradox?
3. How might relativists respond to the charge that their theory is self-refuting?
4. What do you think a paradox tells us about human language and the structure of thought?
5. Describe a time when you noticed someone contradicting him- or herself. Have you ever caught yourself in a contradiction?

Exercises

1. Write a dialogue between Sean and Juanita. Sean argues Sarah wins the court case in the lawyer paradox. Juanita argues in favor of Dr. Peters.
2. Construct a thought experiment to test the claim that relativism promotes peace.

Activities

1. Draw a paradoxical picture.
2. Write a song about tolerance.
3. Watch the movie *The Matrix* (1999), directed by Andy and Larry Wachowski. How does it reflect Descartes' evil genius question?

Community Action Steps

1. Join an organization, such as United Nation's Educational, Scientific, and Cultural Organization (UNESCO), that works for world peace.
2. Visit various different religious centers in your area to learn about their contrasting beliefs.
3. Make banners at your school encouraging tolerance.

References

Descartes, R. (1980). *Meditations on first philosophy* (D. Cress, Trans.). Indianapolis, IN: Hackett. (Original work published 1641)

Wilson, E. O., Rorty, R., & Gross, P. R. (1998). Is everything relative? A debate on the unity of knowledge. *The Wilson Quarterly, 22*(1), 14–49.

Further Reading

Bruce, C. (1997). *The Einstein paradox and other science mysteries solved by Sherlock Holmes.* New York: Perseus Books.

Clark, M. (2002). *Paradoxes from A to Z.* New York: Routledge.

Dennett, D. C. (1999). Why getting it right matters. *Free Inquiry, 20*(1), 40–43.

Descartes, R. (1980). *Meditations on first philosophy* (D. Cress, Trans.). Indianapolis, IN: Hackett. (Original work published 1641)

Gardner, M. (1990). *The snark puzzle book.* Amherst, NY: Prometheus.

Martin, R. M. (2002). *There are two errors in the the title of this book: A sourcebook of philosophical puzzles, problems, and paradoxes.* Orchard Park, NY: Broadview Press.

Nickell, J. (1989). *The magic detectives: Join them in solving strange mysteries.* Orchard Park, NY: Prometheus.

Sorell, T. (2000). *Descartes: A very short introduction.* New York: Oxford University Press.

Sutherland, J. (2000). *The literary detective: 100 puzzles in classic fiction.* Oxford, England: Oxford University Press.

Wilson, E. O., Rorty, R., & Gross, P. R. (1998). Is everything relative? A debate on the unity of knowledge. *The Wilson Quarterly, 22*(1), 14–49.

CHAPTER 6
Is Lying Always Wrong?

The Lie

Shaniqua is sitting on a rock outside of school staring off into space. She doesn't even notice Alex walk up until he snaps his fingers at her.

ALEX: What's up with you, girl?

SHANIQUA: Nothing . . . <*Looking up at him*> I'm getting ready to call my cousin. I promised to help her babysit tonight, but I'm thinking of canceling.

ALEX: Why?

SHANIQUA: <*Looking embarrassed*> Mike asked me over to study, and I'd rather do that.

ALEX: So, what's the problem?

SHANIQUA: Well, I don't want to tell my cousin I'm going to Mike's instead, because she'll be hurt. I'm tempted to tell her I'm sick or something.

ALEX: Hey, as far as I'm concerned, if it's for a good reason it isn't a lie.

SHANIQUA: <*She pauses to think about what Alex said.*> I wish that were true, Alex, but how could it be? It's still a lie. Who decides whether studying with Mike is a good enough reason to break a promise anyway?

ALEX: <*Shaking his head*> Shaniqua, you shouldn't worry about it because your cousin's never going to find out that you lied.

SHANIQUA: So, you think lying's wrong only if you get caught?

ALEX: <*Scratching his head*> Yeah, that's about right.

SHANIQUA: I don't think it matters whether you get caught or not. I think lying's wrong because you're breaking a good rule. I mean, just think how crazy the world would be if there were no rules against lying and everybody lied whenever they felt like it. Would you want to live in a world like that?

ALEX: I would if people used good judgment when they lied. For example, ask me right now whether I like your shirt.

SHANIQUA: <*Smirking*> Do you like my shirt?

ALEX: Yeah, it looks nice.

SHANIQUA: You're lying, aren't you?

ALEX: You bet I am. I'm telling you, Shaniqua, there are some things it's better not to know. Why do you wanna go and hurt your cousin's feelings?

SHANIQUA: Sometimes it's really hard to know what to do. <*She shrugs and shares a smile with Alex.*>

Questions

- When does Alex think lying is OK? Why does Shaniqua think lying is wrong? With which person do you agree more, and why?
- Do you think there can be a good reason for a lie? Why or why not?
- Describe an example of a lie that was wrong. Suppose someone did not think it was wrong. How would you explain to her why you thought it was?

Lying

Is it ever OK to lie? Is a lie ever morally required? If the answer to either of these questions is "yes," then what are we to make of the ninth Biblical commandment, "Thou shalt not bear false witness," or the rule we often hear from parents and teachers, "Honesty is the best policy"?

In this chapter, we'll look at the ethics of lying through the lenses of two of the most influential ethical theories in the history of philosophy. The first is centered on the idea that the moral worth of an action depends on its results. It is called *utilitarianism,* and later we will look at a classic version of utilitarianism defended by John Stuart Mill. This theory says that, of the possible actions open to you, you should choose the one that will do the greatest good for the greatest number, that is, the one that will maximize happiness. The other theory is that morality is based on rights and duties. It is known as *deontology*. This theory says that we are required to perform certain moral duties regardless of the consequences.

Truthfulness is a virtue; there is no denying it. We admire the first American president, George Washington, because, as the story goes, when asked by his father whether he had cut down the cherry tree on the family's property, he responded, "I cannot tell a lie. I cut down the cherry tree." Things are not always so clear-cut, though, as the following examples illustrate:

1. You have a date for a formal dance. You dress up in your finest clothes and greet him when he arrives at your door. He asks, "How do I look?" The truth is that he looks foolish. His suit does not fit right—the sleeves are too short, and the pants are too long. Furthermore, his hair is totally overdone. What do you tell him? If you were in his position, would you want to know the truth?

2. Your favorite great aunt, Veronica, a widow, has a beloved dog named Fifi. Today Fifi was hit by a car and killed. Aunt Veronica, long ill with cancer, is in the hospital and the doctors say she will not survive the night. You know this will be your last visit with her, and she asks how Fifi is. Do you tell her the truth? If you were in her place, would you want to know?

John Stuart Mill (1806–1873) was an English philosopher who learned Greek by age 3 and Latin and math by age 8. His father kept him isolated from other children so he could pursue these studies. At the end of his teenage years, he suffered a nervous breakdown from studying too much. Fortunately, he recovered and went on to a successful career, publishing books about ethics, science, logic, and political economy. He strongly believed philosophy could help improve society in many concrete ways. He ran for office in the English Parliament so that he could make laws reflecting philosophical principles. He also wrote one of the first treatises defending equal rights for women. His works on political liberty and on ethical theory are still widely read and discussed today.

Although it may not be clear what to do in these situations, many think it is clear that the decision should be based not on some abstract rule, but on careful consideration of the consequences of the proposed actions. To take action without considering what will happen seems heartless and inhumane. So, these two examples make a powerful case in favor of the first "results theory" of morality, and also in favor of lying in certain special circumstances.

John Stuart Mill is known as the father of this theory of morality. He would argue that you can find the right thing to do in each of the above situations by determining exactly who will be affected by your choice (including yourself) and calculating which choice will make everyone happy. Mill wanted his theory to be a practical guide to decision making that accurately reflects the way good people instinctively act.

Nevertheless, there are a few problems with Mill's view. First of all, Mill said that the right action is the action that produces the greatest happiness. But, how should we define happiness? Is it wealth, health, fame, glory, or something else? Happiness seems like a very vague concept on which to base a theory. And, Mill's theory seems overly demanding. Many of your moral decisions affect people about whom you know nothing. How will you take them into account? And, how far down the road do you have to look? Most of us have trouble calculating the consequences of our actions for next weekend, never mind next year. Third, and most importantly, it is difficult for Mill's theory to accommodate basic human rights, as the following thought experiment illustrates.

Immanuel Kant (1724–1804) championed the second ethical theory, which says that there are some absolute moral rules. Kant argued in favor of this "rule theory" on the grounds that obeying rules is required to show respect for individual rights. He wanted everyone to obey commands such as "Thou shalt not kill," "Thou shalt not bear false witness," and "Thou shalt protect the innocent," without trying to calcu-

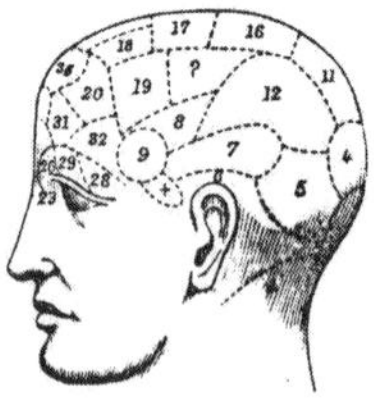

Thought Experiment:
The Mob and the Scapegoat

On a hot summer evening, Juan is driving through a Midwestern city where two racially motivated murders have just occurred. Mobs have formed, and it looks as if there will be riots with severe loss of life if nothing is done. The chief of police knows the mobs will disperse if they have a scapegoat—anyone will do. He has just stopped Juan for running a red light. If he turns Juan over to the mob as the scapegoat, they will kill him, but then disperse. If he lets Juan go, there will be a riot causing dozens of deaths. If we think just in terms of results, it seems we should require the chief of police to sacrifice Juan for the greater good. Does this seem right?

late what will happen. For Kant, the only thing that matters is that you set your mind on doing your duty; the results are not relevant. Because this theory does not attempt to maximize happiness, it avoids the three problems with Mill's theory discussed above.

Despite its merits, Kant's theory has a serious conceptual difficulty. Kant seemed to think that his absolute rules always clearly command one action. But, that just isn't true. Consider what is known as the Anne Frank case (for more on Anne Frank, see p. 56):

> During the Nazi occupation of your country, you are hiding a number of Jewish people behind a false wall in your attic. You know the Nazi secret police are trying to round up these people to murder them. A Nazi officer knocks at your door and asks if you are hiding any Jews in the attic. What should you say?

According to Kant's theory, you have a duty to tell the truth to the officer, but you also have a duty not to cause the death of innocent people. So, this is a case in which our apparent duties conflict.

Yet, Kant addressed cases like this. He seems to think that allowing someone to be killed is not the same as causing their death. According to his theory, if the Nazis come to your door, and there are Jews in your attic, you must tell the truth, because once you leave the attic, you have no idea whether the Jews stayed there or instead ran out the back door to the alley. Suppose they ran out the back door to the alley. You decide you want to save them by lying, but you think they are still in the attic. So, you tell the Nazis to go look in the alley. By lying you have accidentally become the cause of their death; your intention to save their lives has backfired. In other words, you cannot determine what is right or wrong by trying to calculate results. Telling the truth is the only way of preserving your moral integrity in this situation.

This solution is clever, but somewhat paradoxical. The paradox is simply that, for all his talk of ignoring consequences in moral decision making, in his theory Kant has to resort to possible consequences in order to motivate his claim that we should tell the truth to the killers. Do you think there is a solution to this paradox?

It seems obvious from the cases we've considered in this chapter that both moral theories form important parts of our ordinary, day-to-day moral reasoning. Yet, these theories were developed

Immanuel Kant (1724-1804) was a German philosopher who is said to have been a man of very orderly habits. It is said that people could set their watches by when he passed on his daily walk. His three most important books are *Critique of Pure Reason*, *Critique of Practical Reason*, and *Critique of Judgment*. The first explores nature of the human mind. Kant disagreed with Socrates' view that we are born with innate knowledge. But, he also disagreed with Hume's view that all knowledge must come from sense experience. Instead, he believed that, while knowledge must come from experience, our ideas are not exact copies of what is out there. Rather, our minds give order and structure to the raw data of experience. Kant's second book deals with ethics, and the third book deals with art and beauty.

Some philosophical questions have a direct bearing on real-life situations. Anne Frank (1929–1945) was a young Jewish girl living in Amsterdam when the Nazi secret police began capturing all of the Jewish people they could find in order to send them to their concentration camps either as slave labor, or if they were too young, too old, or too sick, simply to execute them. She and her family had to hide in a secret room above her father's office for many months. While she was there she wrote a diary of her experience. The Nazis eventually found and captured her. She died in 1945, just months before her 16th birthday of typhus in Bergen-Belsen, a concentration camp. The people who knew she was hiding faced a very difficult moral dilemma.

in opposition to one another. Do you think there is a way to combine them?

Discussion Questions

1. Review the dialogue at the beginning of this chapter. Does Shaniqua agree more with Kant or Mill? What about Alex? Give evidence.
2. Construct a real-life example where you think it's OK to lie. How would you defend yourself if you got caught?
3. Name two duties or moral obligations that you think might conflict sometimes. How would you resolve the conflict? Can you think of another set of circumstances where you think you might lean toward choosing the other duty?
4. We have focused on lying as an example of a moral rule that may not be absolute. Can you think of any rules that are absolute? If so, try to construct a counterexample to that rule, analogous to the Anne Frank counterexample to the lying rule.
5. Do you think we need to know ethical theory in order to settle practical ethical questions?

Exercises

1. Write a dialogue between Chinelo and Alia. Chinelo argues that we must always consider the consequences of our actions in order to judge whether the actions are ethical or not. Alia argues that, because we are not very good at figuring out what the consequences of our actions will be, we should just live according to a set of ethical rules (such as the Ten Commandments).
2. Construct a thought experiment to test the claim that cheating on a test is always wrong.

Activities

1. Read *Anne Frank: The Diary of a Young Girl,* the diary that Anne Frank wrote while she was in hiding.
2. Watch the movie *Schindler's List* (1993), directed by Steven Spielberg. Was Schindler a follower of the results theory or the rule theory?
3. Watch advertisements on television for instances of lying. What would Mill and Kant say about them?
4. Watch the news for instances of deception in the corporate world and in the government. Are they always wrong?
5. Watch *Groundhog Day* (1993), directed by Harold Ramis. Do you think the main character's lies are wrong?

Community Action Steps

1. Organize a protest against someone who incites hate against a person or a group of people by lying about them.
2. Organize a group to write a letter to the editor of your local newspaper to expose a lie told by a politician.
3. Organize a petition concerning the government's policies on truth in advertising.

References

Frank, A. (1998). *Anne Frank: The diary of a young girl.* New York: Scholastic. (Original work published 1947)

Kant, I. (1956). *Groundwork for the metaphysic of morals* (H. J. Paton, Trans.). New York: Harper and Row. (Original work published 1785)

Mill, J. S. (2002). *Utilitarianism.* Indianapolis, IN: Hackett. (Original work published 1863)

Further Reading

Bok, S. (1999). *Lying: Moral choice in public and private life.* New York: Vintage Books.

Dennett, D. C. (2001). Faith in the truth. *Free Inquiry, 21*(1), 40–42.

Frank, A. (1998). *Anne Frank: The diary of a young girl.* New York: Scholastic. (Original work published 1947)

Kant, I. (1956). *Groundwork for the metaphysic of morals* (H. J. Paton, Trans.). New York: Harper and Row. (Original work published 1785)

Kupfer, J. (1982). The moral presumption against lying. *Review of Metaphysics, 36*(1), 103–126.

Lewis, M., & Saarni, C. (Eds.) (1993). *Lying and deception in everyday life.* New York: Guilford Press.

Mill, J. S. (2002). *Utilitarianism.* Indianapolis, IN: Hackett. (Original work published 1863)

Mills, C. (1999). "Passing": The ethics of pretending to be what you are not. *Social Theory and Practice, 25,* 29–51.

Nuyen, A. T. (1999). Lying and deceiving: Moral choice in public and private life. *International Journal of Applied Philosophy, 13,* 69–79.

Paterno, S. (1997). The lying game. *American Journalism Review, 19,* 40–45.

CHAPTER 7

Does Every Question Have an Answer?

The Brother

Bill meets Lauren at the corner on the way to school. He notices that she seems upset. He pulls two granola bars out of his backpack and offers one to her. Still grumpy, she accepts it and they eat as they walk.

LAUREN: <*Sighing loudly*> I'm so mad at Julie! She's always taking my stuff without permission, and if I tell on her, she twists things with my parents so I get into trouble.

BILL: Just be glad you have a sister. You might have some bad times, but there are bound to be good times, too. Being an only child, I'm just lonely.

LAUREN: <*Thinking about what Bill said for a minute*> I guess you're right, but sometimes I wish I had a brother instead of a sister.

BILL: I'd take either. Sometimes I like to imagine what they would be like.

LAUREN: <*Cheering up a little*> If you had a brother, would he be older or younger than you?

BILL: Younger, so I could be the boss.

LAUREN: Mine would be older, so he could drive me around.

BILL: Would your imaginary brother be tall and play basketball?

LAUREN: Nah, I hate basketball.

BILL: No, but I mean what about him? What would be his favorite team?

LAUREN: <*Growing impatient*> He doesn't have a favorite team!

BILL: But, suppose he did like basketball, then he would have to have a favorite team, right?

LAUREN: No, he wouldn't, 'cause he's my imaginary brother and I get to make him however I want.

BILL: No you don't. There are limits on what kinds of things can exist. <*He pauses to think about it.*> For example, you can't make him 10 feet tall, and you can't make him fly, and because most boys like basketball, he should have a favorite team.

LAUREN: <*Turning grumpy again*> Well, there may be limits on what can exist, but there is no limit on the imagination. If I can't make my imaginary brother how I want him, then I'm just going to imagine him right out of existence.

BILL: <*Shaking his head in frustration*> Great. Meanwhile, I'll try to imagine you being cheerful instead of grumpy for a change.

Questions

- Why does Bill think Lauren's imaginary brother has to have a favorite team? Why does Lauren deny it? With whom do you agree more and why?
- Bill says his imaginary brother is younger than him and Lauren says her imaginary brother is older than her. Are these facts or opinions or neither? Why?
- Is Lauren right when she says there are no limits to what we can imagine? For example, can you imagine one brother who is both older than you and younger than you at the same time?

Do All Questions Have Answers?

Here's a good question for you: What's the opposite of a duck?

Here are some more interesting questions: How much does Thursday weigh? Do curious blue ideas sleep furiously? What is Snow White's father's name? If you could travel back in time 100 years, where would you live? Have you stopped beating your horse?

These are the sorts of questions you might find on a test in a nightmare before a real test at school. Is there a good way to answer any of them? Although they are all grammatically correct, there's something wrong with them.

Look at the first three questions again. Each of these questions contains a type of error that philosophers call category mistakes. A *category mistake* describes something as the wrong kind of thing. A duck is not the kind of thing that can have an opposite, nor can Thursday have weight. And, although the third sentence sounds cool, ideas are not in the category of things that can have color or be asleep. So, questions that involve category mistakes cannot have an answer. Philosophers are interested in examples like these because they show what sometimes goes wrong in a more subtle way when we talk to one another. A lot of philosophical problems are caused by category mistakes.

The next two questions from our list are a bit different. If Snow White's father were in the fairy tale, then presumably he would have a name. And, if you did travel back in time, you would have to live somewhere. So, it seems that these questions can have an answer, but there's no one right answer to either of them. These are examples of what are called *counterfactual conditionals*. Let's call them "what-if" questions. What-if questions help us think about what the world would be like if certain things turned out to be true. For example, if, contrary to fact, Lauren had a brother, then he would like basketball. Or, maybe not.

In addition to being fun to think about, what-if questions also have philosophical significance because they play a crucial role in problem solving. For example, they can help us develop the moral imagination necessary for acting ethically and addressing injustices.

Martha Nussbaum (1947–) is an American philosopher and legal scholar. In her book, *Poetic Justice: The Literary Imagination and Public Life*, she argues that encouraging people to develop

Martha Craven Nussbaum (1947-) is the Ernst Freund Distinguished Service Professor of Law and Ethics at the University of Chicago Law School. She is also the founder and Coordinator of the Center for Comparative Constitutionalism. Nussbaum completed a B.A. at New York University, and received her Ph.D. from Harvard University. She has taught philosophy and classics at Harvard, Brown, and Oxford. Her well-received books include *The Fragility of Goodness* (1986), *Poetic Justice* (1996), *Cultivating Humanity: A Classical Defense of Reform in Liberal Education* (1997), and *Women and Human Development* (2000). Nussbaum is active in a number of organizations devoted to human rights and social justice, and has collaborated with the economist Amartya Sen on the issues of poverty and development, particularly in the developing countries.

their moral imagination is the best way to motivate social reform. She presents two examples of novels that enable the reader to imagine themselves in someone else's shoes. By imaging that we are the characters in these stories, we learn how to sympathize with our fellow human beings.

Nussbaum's first example is *Hard Times*, in which Charles Dickens shows what goes wrong in a society organized on principles of economic efficiency. In imagining such a society, we see its tragic flaws, and because we empathize with the characters, we are moved to correct similar flaws in our own world. *Hard Times* vividly demonstrates why valuing money over love destroys people's sense of self-worth.

Nussbaum's second example is Richard Wright's *Native Son*, the story of a young African American man named Bigger Thomas, who lives in desperate conditions in the Chicago slums. Nussbaum often assigns this book to her classes at the University of Chicago Law School, which is located only 500 yards from the very slums the novel depicts. All of the students know that there are slums nearby where poverty, violence, and drug abuse are common, but reading *Native Son* helps them understand why it is so hard for the people who live there to avoid getting into trouble. Having the students imagine themselves in Bigger's circumstances will not only make these students better lawyers and judges, it will make them better people who are more likely to work for social change. Imagining oneself in the situation of others may be the most effective means of achieving clarity of thought about ethical issues.

We think in terms of "what if" almost everyday. Suppose you want to skip school today. You might say to yourself, "If I skip school today, I'll probably be suspended." This may prevent you from skipping school. In cases like this, you are contemplating alternative realities, or what philosophers call possible worlds. A *possible world* is an imaginary life, related to real life, but having some important differences. We can usefully speak of possible worlds as being farther from or nearer to our actual world, based on how much the imaginary life resembles real life. For example, a possible world in which Lauren has a brother who likes basketball is not very far away, while a possible world in which she has a brother who can fly is quite far away. Good fiction might be described as the creation of a possible world that is near enough for us to relate to it, but far enough away to inspire our imagination.

Are some worlds impossible to imagine? Recall that Bill does not think it possible for Lauren's counterfactual brother to dislike basketball. But, Lauren claims it is possible. Are there any limits to the imagination or rules about what we can imagine? The eminent American philosopher David K. Lewis (1941–2003) thinks there are such rules. For example, Lewis believes that time travel is logically possible, but probably not physically possible. The logical possibility is what allows us to construct possible worlds in which we travel back and forth in time.

Could you travel back in time and kill your grandmother before your mother was born? If you did that, you wouldn't exist. And, if you didn't exist, how could you travel back in time to do the killing? This is a paradox and it leads Lewis to conclude that this sort of world is impossible—so distant from our world that it is unreachable. Maybe there are other less obvious things you cannot do while time traveling, as the following thought experiment suggests.

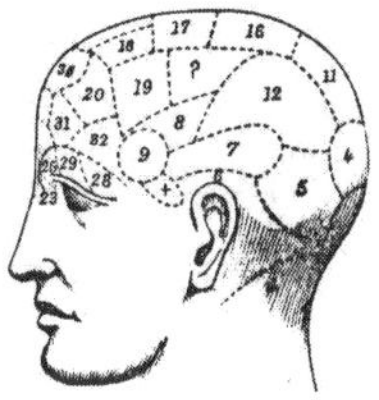

Thought Experiment:
Time Traveling Yourself Out of Existence

Imagine you've been studying the history of warfare in the 20th century. Then you travel back in time to 1939 and tell someone how the Nazis could win World War II. Suppose your information is overheard by someone else who becomes a Nazi general and uses it to actually win World War II for the Nazis. Suppose further that your mother dies as a result of the Nazi victory before giving birth to you. Well, if you are never born then you could never have traveled back in time to give away the information that causes you not to be born. Here we have another version of the time travel paradox.

What about the last question on the list at the beginning of this chapter? Let's assume you do not have a horse. Then, what do you say to someone who asks you: "Have you stopped beating your horse?" If you have to answer "yes" or "no," then you are in bind. If you answer yes, then you seem to be admitting that you used to beat your horse. If you answer no, then you imply that you are still beating your horse. The correct response, of course, is to point out that you do not have a horse. This is to say that the question has a false presupposition. Someone makes a *false presupposition* when they assume something that is not true. False presuppositions are often used deliberately in advertising and can be manipulative. Imagine an ad that depicts a bunch of different types of people, each drinking a different type of Coke—classic, diet, vanilla, lime, etc. The voiceover says: "Which type of person are you?" This ad presupposes that everyone likes Coke. Similarly, suppose your dad asks you whether you would like to go to the

C. S. Peirce (1839–1914) was an American philosopher who, even though he wrote a lot of very good philosophy, could not hold down a job at a university. He mostly worked as a coastal surveyor instead. Until the advent of satellite photography, many maps of the Atlantic coastline were based on those drawn by Peirce. Two of his articles, "The Fixation of Belief" and "How to Make Our Ideas Clear," are seminal pieces in the pragmatist philosophy. The two other most famous classical American pragmatists are William James (1842–1910) and John Dewey (1859–1952). James, who taught at Harvard University, was a more successful academic than Peirce, and did a lot to popularize pragmatism. Dewey worked primarily in education reform. His influence is still strongly felt in the American school system.

movies or to the ballgame this weekend. This presupposes that you want to spend time with him this weekend, when in fact, you may prefer to make plans with someone else.

Even a simple name can contain a presupposition. We have all seen bumper stickers that read "I'm pro-choice" or "I'm pro-life." These statements express opposing points of view on abortion. The pro-choice point of view says that abortion should be legal. The pro-life point of view says abortion should be illegal. Most people have a view about whether abortion should be legal or illegal. But, the names "pro-choice" and pro-life" make it hard to say "no" to either view. If you say "no" to pro-choice, it sounds as though you are against choice. If you say "no" to pro-life, it sounds as though you are against life. But, choice and life are both good things, and no one wants to be against either of them. The way the views are named, you can't win. So, no matter which side you are on, you will have to use a different name for the view you are against. This shows how presuppositions make some questions hard to answer.

Pragmatism is a philosophy especially concerned with unanswerable questions. It was first formulated in the 19th century by Charles Sanders Peirce. Peirce believed that if a question has no practical implications, if it makes no difference in the way you act, then it is a question without an answer and so it should be thrown away.

For example, the philosopher René Descartes famously asked how you know whether or not your whole life is a dream (for more about Descartes, see p. 45). Descartes' attempt to answer this question has vast implications for his entire philosophy. But, because it would not make any difference to our lives whether we were dreaming or not, Peirce rejected this question, along with its alleged implications. According to Peirce, we do not have to answer Descartes, because he is not asking a real question. Pragmatists argue that many philosophers get into trouble by asking answerless questions.

But, there is a price to be paid for this solution: It makes truth dependent on us. If something is not relevant to our lives, then it isn't true *for us*. So the question arises, does pragmatism reduce to relativism? (For more about relativism, see Chapter 5.)

Peirce, at least, didn't think so. He believed that truth consists in what, as a practical matter, we agree upon, and he defined this agreement counterfactually. Truth is what we would all accept were we to have the time, resources, and ingenuity to answer all of our questions to our satisfaction. Of course, we will never answer all of our questions because each new answer seems to generate new questions, and so we will probably never reach the truth. That does not mean that progress is impossible, however. Consider this analogy: Probably none of us will ever become a saint, but sainthood can still be an ideal goal, and we can all still become better people.

So, we've discovered that when it comes to questions, things are not always as they appear. Watch for tricks like these in your daily life. You may be surprised how often they come up and how much trouble they can cause.

Discussion Questions

1. Construct your own examples of questions that contain category mistakes. For each one, say what the mistake is.
2. Choose a period in the past that you would like to visit. Describe the time and place, and any people you would like to meet. Say what you would try to change about this time. Are there any things you think you would logically be prevented from doing?
3. How do you think a pragmatist would respond to questions such as "Is there intelligent life on other planets?" or "What will our solar system be like after our Sun dies out?"
4. Do you think it is good to set goals that you'll probably never reach? Why or why not?
5. Have you ever read a novel or watched a movie that enabled you to empathize with someone else's problems? Explain.

Exercises

1. Write a dialogue between Darci and Onora. Darci argues that philosophers never answer any questions. Onora argues that they do.
2. Construct a thought experiment to test the claim that it is possible to travel to the future.

Activities

1. Find examples of advertisements that rely on false presuppositions.
2. Write a poem that uses category mistakes to convey a paradoxical emotion.
3. Watch the movie *Terminator* (1984), directed by James Cameron. Are there paradoxes in this story? Explain.
4. Watch the movie *Waking Life* (2001), directed by Richard Linklater. Is the lead character pursuing questions that cannot be answered? What does he learn along the way?

Community Action Steps

1. Read a work of literature with a younger relative.
2. Invite an author to your school to discuss the role of moral imagination in his or her work.
3. Volunteer at an inner-city community center.

References

Nussbaum, M. C. (1995). *Poetic justice: The literary imagination and public life.* Boston: Beacon Press.

Pierce, C. S. (1877, November). The fixation of belief. *Popular Science Monthly, 12,* 1–15.

Further Reading

Arthur, C. (1995). Zen and the art of asking questions. *Contemporary Review, 267,* 253–257.

Martin, R. M. (2002). *There are two errors in the the title of this book: A sourcebook of philosophical puzzles, problems, and paradoxes.* Orchard Park, NY: Broadview.

Nussbaum, M. C. (1995). *Poetic justice: The literary imagination and public life.* Boston: Beacon Press.

Pierce, C. S. (1877, November). The fixation of belief. *Popular Science Monthly, 12,* 1–15.
Skidelsky, E. (2002, June 17). The human question-mark. *New Statesman, 131,* 48–51.

CHAPTER 8
Should We Accept Reality?

The Athlete

Dakota is sitting in the locker room putting on his shoes for football practice. Tony walks in wearing a tank top and shorts. He is very muscular.

DAKOTA: Hey Tony, I haven't seen you since last spring. Have you been hittin' the gym all summer? How'd you get so buff?

TONY: Yeah, hittin' the gym with a little help from my friends here. <*He pulls out a packet of pills.*> You want some? Man, you look like you could use it! <*He offers the packet to Dakota.*>

DAKOTA: <*Surprised*> What is that, steroids? You've got to be kidding!

TONY: <*Defensive*> It's nothing illegal. It's just a way to enhance your performance.

DAKOTA: Tony, you're not enhancing your performance, you're cheating. Athletes are supposed to play fair.

TONY: Oh, come on! You don't think the guys on the other teams aren't taking these? I'm telling you, it's the only way to win. <*He grins.*> I like to win.

DAKOTA: That's not what sports is about to me. It's about achieving to the best of your ability. Taking pills makes it all just a game.

TONY: <*Tony walks over to his locker and opens it, shaking his head.*> How can you say sports isn't a game?

DAKOTA: Well, but it's not *just* a game. It's like life. It tests your strength and your commitments. It reveals who you really are—what you're made of. I feel like if I won a game on steroids, it wouldn't be real.

TONY: Believe me, it feels just as real—in fact, it's better than real. Everybody has to do something to make life more fun. Some people drink, some people smoke, some people pray . . .

DAKOTA: Yeah, and some people are happy with life just the way it is.

TONY: <*Walking away, looking back over his shoulder*> Boring!

Questions

- What is the purpose of sports according to Dakota? What is its purpose according to Tony? With whom do you agree more, and why?
- Do you think that taking steroids is a form of cheating? Should professional athletes be permitted to use performance enhancing drugs?
- Have you ever used a drug? Did it make the reality you were experiencing better?
- Why do you think Dakota thinks it would be better to be happy with reality as it is? Do you agree with him?

Reality

The word *philosophy* comes from Greek words meaning "the love of wisdom." Most philosophers are not so bold as to call themselves wise, but by thinking about things and talking to one another about tough issues, they strive to become wiser.

What exactly is wisdom? There are probably a number of different definitions. Most, however, will feature the notion of truth. A wise person would know the truth about life, would not be fooled by false impressions, and certainly would not engage in self-deception. A wise person would be completely in touch with reality.

Considering that wisdom is widely regarded as a good thing, it is amazing that so many people spend so much time and energy trying to *escape* truth and reality. Consider Tony in the dialogue above. He takes steroids because he is not satisfied with the truth about his own natural abilities. There are dozens of other examples. Girls wear make-up to make them look older; women have cosmetic surgery to make them look younger. Both men and women dye their hair, or perm it, or straighten it. They go to tanning booths to darken their skin or apply creams to lighten it. They buy cars and vacuum cleaners that are made to sound more powerful than they really are. They visit restaurants made to look like they are set in another country and theme parks made to look as though they are set in the past or in the future. They go to movies and read books to pretend for a while that they are someone else. Parents believe that *their* children are the only ones who do not engage in bad behavior. We all try to escape reality sometimes. If wisdom means seeking the truth, would it be better for us to accept reality as it is?

According to the ancient Greek philosopher Zeno of Citium (333–264 BC), the answer is yes. Zeno founded the school of thought known as *stoicism* (pronounced stow-icism). A stoic is someone who accepts everything that happens without emotion. Stoics never let themselves feel happy or sad. They try never to react with anger, enthusiasm, or surprise. They go through life with a straight face, ready for anything. We still use the word *stoic* today. For example, a sports announcer might say, "The coach accepted the loss stoically."

Stoic philosophy is often represented in the form of a tree. Logic forms the tree's roots. The trunk of the tree is physics, whose

Zeno of Citium (or Cittium) was born in Cyprus, and moved his school to Athens where he taught at a place called Stoa Poikile, whence the name "stoicism" for his philosophy. (Zeno of Citium is not to be confused with the Zeno whom we met in Chapter 5. That is Zeno of Elea who lived in the fifth century BC.) Very little remains of Zeno's writing, and there are only a few stories about his life. The Athenians sold him into slavery when he couldn't pay a tax required of all foreigners, yet they honored him later in life with a golden crown, and with an elaborate tomb after his death. Zeno is known as the first utopian anarchist in the West and a precursor to today's idea of anarchism. It is also said that he was fond of sitting in the sun, eating figs, and drinking wine.

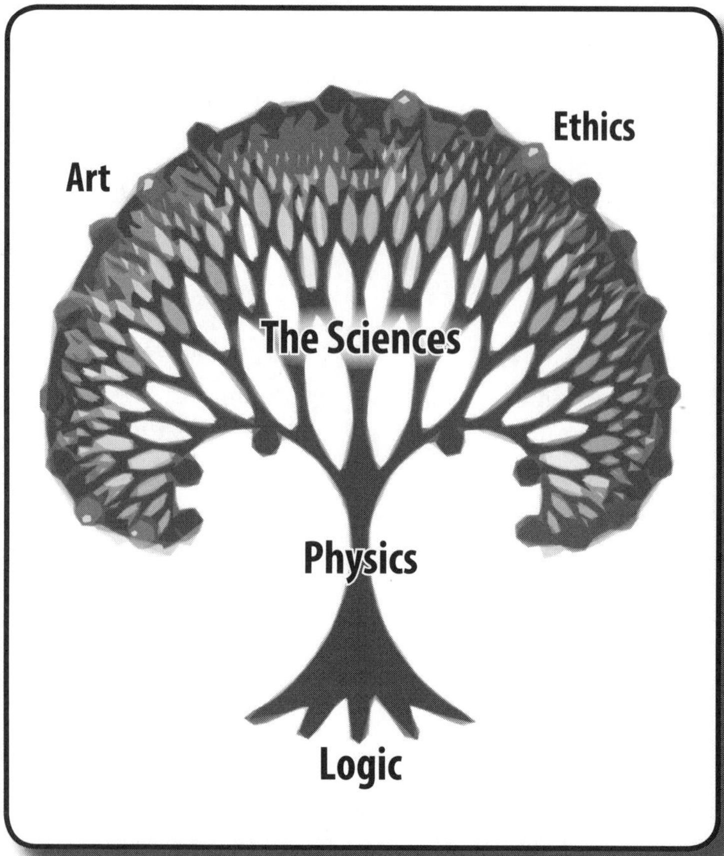

name comes from the Greek word for nature. The branches of the tree are psychology, biology, geology, chemistry, and all of the other sciences. Ethics and art are the fruit of the tree. Notice that the stoic tree is completely free of emotion. Even ethics and art are supported by the laws of physics and fed through the roots of logic.

It is evident that stoicism may be advantageous in certain situations. For example, if you have to do a reading at the funeral of a dear friend, you may stoically suppress your grief so that it does not prevent you from being able to perform. Or, if you win a prize in front of friends who did not win, you may stoically suppress your excitement to avoid making them feel bad. But, true stoics adopt a straight face for all occasions in life. Why would they do that?

Stoics believe all things happen of necessity in accordance with fixed laws of nature. Surprising things *seem* to happen. But, we are only surprised because we are not aware of the necessary principles that caused them to happen. Someone who understood all the laws of nature would never be surprised about anything and could predict the future perfectly. Stoics believe the necessary principles that govern the universe also apply to human actions. Although we seem to make choices that enable us to control our future, this is an illusion. Even our choices are necessitated by the laws of nature. This may seem strange at first, but if you think about it, the science of psychology itself seems to assume that human behavior is predictable.

Zeno developed stoicism in connection with his unique religious views. He wrote,

> God is not separate from the world; He is the soul of the world, and each of us contains a part of the Divine Fire. All things are parts of one single system, which is called Nature; the individual life is good when it is in harmony with Nature. In one sense, every life is in harmony with

> Nature, since it is such as Nature's laws have caused it to be; but in another sense a human life is in harmony with Nature only when the individual will is directed to ends that are among those of Nature. Virtue consists in a will which is in agreement with Nature. The wicked, though perforce they obey God's law, do so involuntarily; in the simile of Cleanthes, they are like a dog tied to a cart, and compelled to go wherever it goes. (From *Stoicism Quotations* [http://www.spaceandmotion.com/Philosophy-Stoicism-Zeno.htm])

Given Zeno's concern to accept reality as it is, he probably would not be in favor of drinking or drug abuse, wearing make-up, or even watching *Spiderman*. Instead of trying to fight nature, and being inevitably dragged along with it, we should peacefully follow its lead. At least if you avoid getting your hopes up too high about life, you will never be too disappointed.

Zeno had a rival named Epicurus (340–271 BC). Epicurus completely rejected Zeno's claims about the laws of nature. According to Epicurus, nature is composed of tiny particles. Most of the time these particles move in the same direction, but sometimes they swerve, creating unpredictable results. Human freedom is also a swerve in nature. Much of what we do follows the lead of nature, but sometimes we make unpredictable choices. Epicurus believed the secret to living a good individual life is making choices that will bring pleasure. He wrote,

> We recognize pleasure as the first good innate in us, and from pleasure we begin every act of choice and avoidance, and to pleasure we return again, using the feeling as the standard by which we judge every good. (From *Letter to Menoeceus* by Epicurus [http://alien.dowling.edu/~cperring/epicurustomenoeceus.html], ¶ 12)

Epicurus was against stoic indifference. In his view, we can control our future and we should try to make it as pleasant as we can.

Epicurus also rejected religion because he felt it makes life unpleasant. When people believe in God (or gods) they spend a great deal of time worrying about how their actions might be judged. Worrying gets in the way of enjoying life, which, for Epicurus, is of the utmost importance.

Because of his emphasis on pleasure and his rejection of religion, Epicurus gained a reputation for endorsing a life of wild partying. In fact, Epicurus was more likely to warn that such behavior would ultimately undermine your ability to enjoy your life because of the various problems it can cause. We are all familiar with the problems associated with overeating, for example. Epicurus has followers, however, known as *hedonists,* who advocate living life to the fullest without regard for conventional morality. Hedonists value food, drink, sex, sleep, and anything else that feels good. They advocate pursuing pleasure in any way you can.

Most ancient Greeks were polytheists, meaning they believed in many gods. One important god was named Bacchus, the god of wine. Hedonists worshipped the god of wine. Interestingly, most ancient Greek philosophers, such as Plato, Aristotle, Zeno, and Epicurus rejected the popular religion of their day. Although they had some religious beliefs, they did not worship these gods. Today most people in Western culture are monotheists, meaning that they believe in only one god (whether the religion is Christianity, Judaism, or Islam). Just like their ancient predecessors, however, many Western philosophers reject popular religion in favor of atheism, which is the belief that there are no gods, or agnosticism, which is a suspension of judgment on the question of the existence of any god. Why do you suppose philosophers have always tended to be critical of popular religion?

The Feast of Bacchus, 1629, Diego Rodriguez de Silva y Velázquez

Is it realistic to see life as the pursuit of pleasure, or is hedonism an attempt to escape reality? To help you consider this question, try the thought experiment on the next page.

Many people would argue that there is much more to reality than pleasure. For example, visiting someone in the hospital is not very pleasant. Yet, it is a nice thing to do. Many would say it is a duty to take care of our loved ones, even though taking care of people often is not much fun. It may involve cooking, cleaning, doing laundry, loaning money, running errands, listening, comforting, and helping in many other ways. Hedonists will not be inclined to do any of these things. Some philosophers think this shows that hedonism is an unacceptably selfish approach to life. The English philosopher John Stuart Mill famously said that it is better to be Socrates than a fool, even if the fool is satisfied with his life and Socrates is not. Mill distinguished between "higher" and "lower" pleasures, arguing that wisdom and truth, even if they are sometimes painful, are always preferable to pleasures gained from self-deception. (For more on this, see the second chapter of his book *Utilitarianism.*)

Thought Experiment: Getting Your Jollies

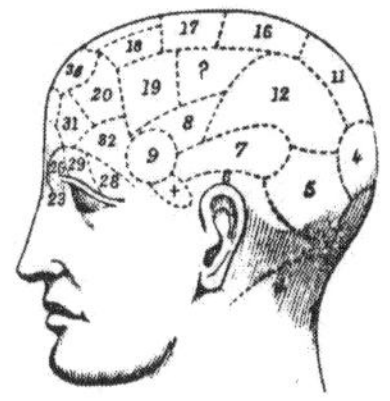

Imagine scientists have mapped out the pleasure centers of the brain, so they know exactly which brain cells "fire" when you experience the pleasures associated with eating and drinking, exercise, sex, etc. Suppose further that the scientists can insert electrodes into your brain and stimulate those brain cells in such a way that it feels exactly like you were experiencing the real thing. They tell you that you can stay attached to the electrodes as long as you want. Do you think you would choose to spend your life attached to the electrodes? Do you think this would be a desirable life? (This experiment has actually been done with rats, and the rats consistently choose electrode stimulation, even if it means foregoing food.)

The question remains: Should we accept reality? Some people say it is OK to escape reality. Others say that if we are not happy with reality, we should change it. In this view, rather than trying to escape the problems in our lives we should solve them and try to improve reality for everyone.

Discussion Questions

1. Review the dialogue at the beginning of this chapter. Is Dakota more of a Stoic or more of an Epicurean? What about Tony? Give evidence.
2. Would Zeno approve of Tony's use of steroids? Why or why not?
3. Do you agree with Zeno that the laws of nature necessitate everything you do or do you agree with Epicurus that your actions are free?
4. How might a hedonist respond to the charge that his view is unacceptably selfish?
5. List some ways you think it is OK to escape reality and some ways you think it is not OK.

Exercises

1. Write a dialogue between Skylar and Dante. Skylar argues that professional athletes should be allowed to use performance-enhancing drugs, even if it will eventually harm them. He argues that it is the athletes' right to choose, just as any of us can choose to harm ourselves by smoking and drinking. Dante denies this. He argues that this use will spread to children and really cause a lot of harm.
2. Construct a thought experiment to test the claim that human beings naturally seek pleasure.

Activities

1. Draw a picture of some aspect of reality you do not like. Then, draw a picture of how you would like it to be instead.
2. Try giving up caffeine for one month. (Remember: Chocolate contains caffeine.)
3. Watch the movie *Basketball Diaries* (1995), directed by Scott Kalvert. What do you think it is trying to say about athletes and drug addiction?
4. Form a group to read and discuss the books *Clockwork Orange,* by Anthony Burgess, or *Siddhartha,* by Hermann Hesse. How does a human being become good according to these books?

Community Action Steps

1. Volunteer to work a Special Olympics competition.
2. Volunteer at a substance abuse clinic.
3. Join a D.A.R.E. program.
4. Organize a Smoke Free Day at your school.

References

Epicurus. (n.d.) *Letter to Menoeceus.* Retrieved on January 2, 2006, from http://alien.dowling.edu/~cperring/epicurustomenoeceus.html (Original work written 306–270 BC)

Mill, J. S. (1998). *Utilitarianism.* Indianapolis, IN: Hackett. (Original work published 1863)

Spaceandmotion.com. (n.d.). *Stoicism quotations.* Retrieved on January 2, 2006, from http://www.spaceandmotion.com/Philosophy-Stoicism-Zeno.htm

Further Reading

Annas, J. (1995). *The morality of happiness.* New York: Oxford University Press.

Darnton, R. (1995). The pursuit of happiness. *The Wilson Quarterly, 19*(4), 42–52.

Epicurus. (n.d.) *Letter to Menoeceus.* Retrieved on Janauary 2, 2006, from http://alien.dowling.edu/~cperring/epicurustomenoeceus.html (Original work written 306–270 BC)

Hicks, R. (1961). *Stoic and epicurean.* New York: Russell & Russell.

Inwood, B. (1985). *Ethics and human action in early stoicism.* Oxford, England: Clarendon Press.

Kingwell, M. (2001). What does it all mean? *The Wilson Quarterly, 25*(2), 35–43.

Mill, J. S. (1998). *Utilitarianism.* Indianapolis, IN: Hackett. (Original work published 1863)

Morgan, W. J., Meier, K. V., & Schneider, A. (Eds.). (2001). *Ethics in sport.* Champaign, IL: Human Kinetics.

Pink, T. (2004). *Free will: A very short introduction.* New York: Oxford.

Spaceandmotion.com. (n.d.). *Stoicism quotations.* Retrieved on January 2, 2006, from http://www.spaceandmotion.com/Philosophy-Stoicism-Zeno.htm

PART 3

Justice

The Stanza della Segnatura Ceiling: Justice, 1509–1511, Raphael

CHAPTER 9
What is Discrimination?

Malcolm X

In his autobiography, the political activist Malcolm X (1925–1965) presents a vivid picture of discrimination when he describes his encounter with a teacher named Mr. Ostrowski as follows:

> He told me, "Malcolm, you ought to be thinking about a career. Have you been giving it thought?" The truth is, I hadn't. I never have figured out why I told him, "Well, yes, sir, I've been thinking I'd like to be a lawyer." In those days, Lansing certainly had no Negro lawyers—or doctors either—to hold up an image I might have aspired to. All I really knew for certain was that a lawyer didn't wash dishes, as I was doing.
>
> Mr. Ostrowski looked surprised, I remember, and leaned back in his chair and clasped his hands behind his head. He kind of half-smiled and said, "Malcolm, one of life's first needs is for us to be realistic about being a nigger. A lawyer—that's no realistic goal for a nigger. You need to think about something you can be. You're good with your hands—making things. Everybody admires your carpentry shop work. Why don't you plan on carpentry? People like you as a person—you'd get all kinds of work."
>
> The more I thought afterward about what he said, the more uneasy it made me. It just kept treading around in my mind. What made it really begin to disturb me was Mr. Ostrowski's advice to others in my class—all

of them white. . . . Some, mostly girls, wanted to be teachers. A few wanted other professions, such as one boy who wanted to become a county agent; another, a veterinarian; and one girl wanted to be a nurse. They all reported that Mr. Ostrowski had encouraged whatever they had wanted. Yet nearly none of them had earned marks equal to mine. (From *The Autobiography of Malcolm X: As Told to Alex Haley*, by Alex Haley and Malcolm X, 1964, p. 37)

Questions

- How does Mr. Ostrowski mistreat Malcolm X? Given that Mr. Ostrowski seems to like Malcolm X, why do you think he mistreats him?
- Describe a time when you have been mistreated by someone who did not notice he or she was mistreating you. How did it make you feel?
- If Mr. Ostrowski had said those things to you, how might you have responded? How do you think Mr. Ostrowski might have defended himself?

Discrimination

The story Malcolm X tells about Mr. Ostrowski in his autobiography depicts racial discrimination. It also shows how we can be discriminatory without a hateful attitude, and without even knowing it. *Discrimination* is a kind of mistreatment. It happens when someone with authority makes you feel inferior or denies you equal rights simply because you belong to a certain group.

If we are going to treat persons or groups differently, we should have a good reason for doing so. Sometimes we do have a good reason. For example, we might not hire someone to be a crossing guard at a school because he has a severe visual impairment. Choosing someone else for the job is legitimate in this case, because the reason is relevant to the person's ability to do the job effectively.

Treating persons or groups differently becomes discriminatory when the reason for the different treatment is not relevant. People of color, women, and gay people are examples of groups that are often discriminated against. Skin color, gender, and sexual preference are not relevant reasons for being treated differently. Even though discrimination is widely recognized as a bad thing, it is very prevalent in our culture. The harmful effect of systematic discrimination is known as *oppression*. It comes from the word *press*, as in pressing someone down or keeping him from achieving success and happiness in life.

Throughout history, governments have been known to make discriminatory laws, or at least tolerate discriminatory practices. For example, in the United States, women were not allowed to vote until the year 1920. Women also were not allowed to do many other things that men were allowed to do. For example, in 1904, a woman was arrested in New York City for smoking a cigarette! (Men had, of course, been smoking cigarettes since they were invented in the 17th century.) To this day, it is illegal for a woman to go topless in most public places, but it is not illegal for men. Do you think this is an instance of discrimination? (The "no topless" law has been successfully challenged in court in Canada.) Although people may not agree as to exactly what counts as discrimination and what does not, there is no question that discrimination still exists in many forms.

Many philosophers and activists today are working hard on the question of what to do to end discrimination once and for all. In

The original name of Malcolm X (1925-1965) was Malcolm Little, who was born in Omaha, NE. He changed his name when he converted to Islam while in prison for petty criminal offenses. His father died when he was relatively young (there were rumors that he was murdered by a White supremacist organization) and his mother was deemed mentally incompetent and had to be institutionalized. Malcolm X and Dr. Martin Luther King, Jr. were the two most prominent leaders in the Civil Rights Movement—the struggle for equality by African Americans. The chief difference between Malcolm X and King is that King preached nonviolent civil disobedience, while Malcolm X argued that violence is a permissible method for achieving racial equality when peaceful methods are not sufficiently effective. Both men were assassinated. Malcolm was shot as he was beginning a speech.

the 1960s, during the Civil Rights Movement, the solution known as affirmative action was introduced. *Affirmative action* requires businesses and schools to ensure that oppressed groups enjoy the same opportunities as everyone else. This means such institutions must make a strong effort to give members of oppressed groups a fair chance when they compete for things such as jobs and scholarships.

Because members of oppressed groups start with a disadvantage, giving them a fair chance may mean giving them special consideration. This may take the form of giving them preferential treatment when their qualifications are no better or no worse than those of other nonminority candidates. Sometimes, when it is clear that the minority person is minimally qualified for a position, it may be awarded to that person even though there are more qualified nonminority candidates.

For example, until recently, students applying for admission to the University of Michigan had to complete a racial preference application. This application required the students to submit all the usual test scores, letters, and transcripts, along with information about their race. The university used a point system to rank the applications; in this system, being Black automatically gave a person more points than being White.

Affirmative action was originally conceived as a temporary remedy that would solve the problem of discrimination and soon become unnecessary. After 40 years, however, affirmative action still has not solved the problem. For example, the percentage of White Americans with university degrees still exceeds the percentage of Black Americans with university degrees. There is a great deal of controversy over whether or not affirmative action is a good solution.

In June of 2003, the Supreme Court issued decisions against racial preference admissions applications. Two cases, called *Gratz et al. v. Bollinger et al.* and *Grutter v. Bollinger et al.,* make the continued use of racial preferences risky for colleges. Schools either have to stop considering race on applications or show that their racial preference policies are not applied mechanically, but only in an individualized way. So, the University of Michigan can continue with affirmative action, but not with a point system.

Cornel West (1953–) is a prominent American philosopher who defends affirmative action. He writes,

> Given the history of this country, it is a virtual certainty that without affirmative action, racial and sexual discrimination would return with a vengeance. Even if affirmative action fails significantly to reduce black poverty or contrib-

> utes to the persistence of racist perceptions in the workplace, without affirmative action, black access to America's prosperity would be even more difficult to obtain and racism in the workplace would persist anyway. (From *Race Matters*, by Cornel West, 1994, p. 95)

Not all African Americans support affirmative action, however. Supreme Court Justice Clarence Thomas is on record as being against affirmative action. Other philosophers also reject affirmative action. Professor Glenn Loury (1948–) is concerned that it is a form of "reverse discrimination." He says,

> Simply put, white male Americans have rights too. How can one justify denying admission to an elite professional school to a working-class white youth of immigrant parents, who has struggled against all odds to be able to score high on the admissions test, while admitting instead a member of an appropriately designated minority group, who has enjoyed all the advantages of an upper-middle-class upbringing—but has not performed as well according to standard admissions criteria? (From *Race and Affirmative Action: An Interview With Professor Glenn Loury of Harvard University*, 1984, ¶ 4)

Loury maintains that we should judge applicants on the basis of their merits rather than focusing on what groups they belong to. Of course, there is another dimension to affirmative action. We are not just concerned with the direct selection of one person over another; if we are going to reduce the need for affirmative action in the future, we need to increase the visible presence of minority role models now. Loury's objection does not address this aspect of affirmative action.

Both West and Loury want equal rights for all

Thought Experiment: Desert Dessert

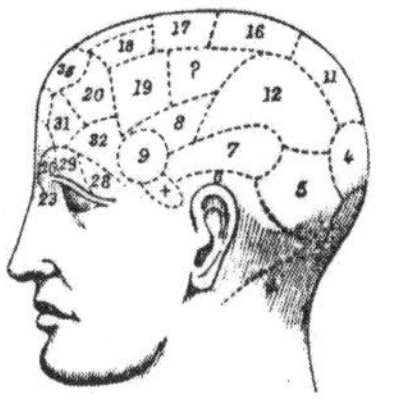

Imagine that you are babysitting a 6-year-old and an 8-year-old. The parents have left some treats for dessert: two bananas, a lollipop, and an ice cream bar. The parents' instructions were to allow each child to choose one treat. Unfortunately, both kids want the ice cream bar. How can you distribute the goods fairly? The easiest way would be to give them each a banana. But, neither wants a banana. Perhaps the older child should have first pick because she has more responsibilities. Or, perhaps the younger child should have first pick because he has less opportunities. Perhaps they should compete for first pick. But, that seems to give the older child an automatic advantage again. Perhaps you could split the ice cream bar in half, but then they should be allowed to split something else, and the only other thing they want is the lollipop, which is hard to split. As you can see, this is a complicated problem. How would you solve it?

Americans, as our Constitution requires, but they disagree about how this equality can be achieved. Achieving equality is a very tricky business, because everyone has different needs and desires. Nevertheless, we all have to make decisions about the distribution of things we value in our daily lives. And, we all want to be fair in these decisions.

Making decisions about fairness on a day-to-day basis may be difficult, but it is easy compared to deciding how to vote. When we vote we are supposed to try to elect the people we believe will distribute the nation's resources fairly. It is tempting, of course, to vote for whichever government will be the best *for you*. But, that would be like eating the ice cream bar yourself and leaving the kids to fight over the lollipop.

John Rawls (1921–2002) is perhaps the most famous American political theorist of the 20th century. In his landmark work, *A Theory of Justice* (1971), he presents a thought experiment that can help us figure out what a fair government is like. He asks you to imagine that you don't know whether you are male or female, Black or White, gay or straight, young or old, rich or poor, and well educated or uneducated. In other words, imagine that you are stripped of every identifying feature other than simply being human. Now, under this "veil of ignorance," choose the government you think would be best. Then, after you make your choice, you must take off the veil of ignorance and find out which type of person you are.

This thought experiment is useful because it helps prevent us from voting for selfish reasons. You would not want to choose a government that discriminates against gays, because when you take off the veil of ignorance, you might find out you that are gay. Rawls also thinks that this thought experiment can help close the gap between the rich and the poor, a gap created by discrimination. He argues that under the veil of ignorance we would adopt what he calls the *difference principle* when we are deciding how goods and services will be distributed in our society. The difference principle says that society should be organized so that even poor people have a chance at a meaningful and happy life. It says that any change in social structure must not benefit the rich if it also makes the poor worse off. Therefore, you would not elect a brutal dictatorship or a society that sanctioned slavery, because you may well end up as a person who isn't very well off. (Remember, when you are choosing a government under the veil of ignorance, you must consider the possibility that you may be poor, a dictator's victim, or a slave.)

Many philosophers think this thought experiment could help us eliminate discrimination and the accompanying disparity of wealth. Many others, however, find problems with it. They claim that it is impossible to imagine yourself without any identifying features. If you do not know who you are, you have no basis for making a choice. This criticism seems to presuppose that all choices stem from selfishness in that we want to benefit the group to which we belong, and that this is not necessarily wrong. Although philosophers disagree over John Rawls' thought experiment, one thing they agree about is that it represents a very creative effort to solve a very important problem.

Discussion Questions

1. Explain an instance when you feel you were the victim of discrimination or reverse discrimination. How would you make your case that what happened was wrong?
2. In most states it is illegal for anyone under the age of 21 to drink alcohol. Do you think this is discrimination? Why or why not?
3. How do you think Malcolm X would respond to Glenn Loury's concern about reverse discrimination?
4. Are you for or against affirmative action? Why?
5. Which kind of government does the veil of ignorance thought experiment cause you to choose? Would you choose a representative democracy, for example, or a direct democracy, or a benevolent dictatorship?

Exercises

1. Write a dialogue between Shanna and Charro. Shanna argues against affirmative action. Charro argues for it.
2. Construct a thought experiment against the claim that reverse discrimination is impossible.

Activities

1. Visit a history museum and write a report about the section devoted to social movements.
2. Watch the news and make a list of current civil rights issues.
3. Watch the movie *Malcolm X* (1992), directed by Spike Lee. Do you find his defense of violence compelling?

Community Action Steps

1. Participate in a political protest.
2. Write a letter to your state representative about a civil rights issue that concerns you.
3. Invite a civil rights activist to speak at your school.
4. Volunteer to help register voters at election time.

References

Cooray, M. (1985). *Race and affirmative action: An interview with professor Glenn Loury of Harvard University.* Retrieved January 27, 2006, from http://www.ourcivilisation.com/cooray/rights/chap17.htm

Haley, A., & X, M. (1965). *The autobiography of Malcolm X: As told to Alex Haley*. New York: Random House.

Rawls, J. (1971). *A theory of justice.* Cambridge, MA: Harvard University Press.

West, C. (1994). *Race matters.* New York: Vintage.

Further Reading

Anderson, B. C. (2003, Spring). The antipolitical philosophy of John Rawls. *Public Interest, 151*, 39–52.

Burns, S. (1993). Martin Luther King, Jr.'s empowering legacy. *Tikkun, 8*(2), 49–56.

Cooray, M. (1985). *Race and affirmative action: An interview with professor Glenn Loury of Harvard University.* Retrieved January 27, 2006, from http://www.ourcivilisation.com/cooray/rights/chap17.htm

Curry, G. E. (1996). *The affirmative action debate.* New York: Perseus Books.

Haley, A., & X, M. (1965). *The autobiography of Malcolm X: As told to Alex Haley.* New York: Random House.

Kly, Y. N., & X, M. (1986). *The Black book: The true political philosophy of Malcolm X.* Atlanta, GA: Clarity Press.

Rawls, J. (1971). *A theory of justice.* Cambridge, MA: Harvard University Press.

West, C. (1994). *Race matters.* New York: Vintage

CHAPTER 10
Do Animals Have Rights?

The Dog

Nelson is walking through an alley. Passing an empty lot, he hears commotion behind a high wall. As he walks toward it, he sees his neighbor Matt and his yellow lab, Viking. Viking is growling and snapping; Matt is trying to grab his collar.

NELSON: What's the matter with your dog, man?

MATT: <*Matt looks up, surprised. On seeing Nelson, he seems a little embarrassed.*> Oh, he's just mad 'cause he hurt himself.

NELSON: <*Coming closer, Nelson can see that the fur on Viking's right leg is matted down and black. It looks singed. Just then, Nelson smells smoke.*> That's too bad. What are you up to, a barbecue?

MATT: Nah. We were just goofin' around.

NELSON: With fire?

MATT: Well, actually, I was trying to see if I could get him to jump through this. <*Matt holds up a burnt hoop.*> You know that show "Amazing Animals"? Well, they're having a dog trick contest. The winner gets $200. Viking jumps through this hoop all the time at home, so I thought I could get him to do it while it was on fire.

<Nelson is beginning to look uncomfortable.>

MATT: *<Matt continues>* But, he won't do it. Stupid chicken dog! Not even for a raw steak. Not even after I didn't feed him for 2 days. *<He glares at Viking, now lying on the other side of the lot, licking his right leg.>*

NELSON: *<Bursting out>* Man! You're mean! I can't believe you did that. You don't have the right to treat an animal that way!

MATT: What are you talking about? The dog is mine. I can do whatever I want with him. He's lucky I don't kick him out of the house for being so stubborn.

NELSON: Just because you own him doesn't mean you can abuse him. That's like saying you can treat a baby however you want just because he's yours.

MATT: No way! It's not like that at all. A baby's human. That makes all the difference. Humans have rights, animals don't.

NELSON: But, why? They both suffer the same. Viking's cryin' like a baby right now.

<They both turn to look at Viking. Nelson looks sad, Matt looks skeptical.>

Questions

- Why does Nelson think animals have rights? Why does Matt think they don't? Who do you agree with more, and why?
- What do you think it means to have rights?
- Describe a time when you saw or heard about someone mistreating an animal. Suppose the person who was doing it told you it was none of your business. Would you try to persuade them to stop in order to save the animal? If not, why? If so, how might you make your case?

Animal Rights

It certainly sounds odd to speak of a chicken's right to life, liberty, and the pursuit of happiness, doesn't it? Some people are inclined to respond that it only makes sense to attribute rights to creatures that can understand the concept of a right. This cannot be true though, because it would imply that young children and mentally handicapped adults have no rights. So, how can we decide whether or not animals have rights? (Strictly speaking, we should use the phrase *nonhuman animals*, because humans are animals, too. But, we will stick with the simpler name, *animals*.)

The English philosopher Jeremy Bentham (1748–1832) insists that "The question is not, Can they reason? nor, Can they talk? but, Can they suffer?" (Bentham, 1780/1970, pp. 282–283). Bentham subscribes to the "results theory" of ethics, which says that we should do whatever produces the greatest happiness for the greatest number. (For more about this theory, known as *utilitarianism*, see Chapter 6.) Notice that it does not say the greatest number of *people*. What is important is the promoting or maximizing of pleasure and the minimizing of pain *wherever it occurs*. Does this mean you should feed a starving dog before you feed a hungry child? Of course not. But, it does mean, according to Bentham, that the dog's suffering should be morally significant to you.

How do we know animals feel pain? Well, strictly speaking, we do not. But then, strictly speaking, we cannot know that for certain about human beings either, can we? However, practically speaking, we never doubt it. We infer that other people feel pain because they behave as we do when we feel pain and because we know they have the same brains and nervous systems as we do. But, we also know that many animals have brains and nervous systems very similar to ours, and when they are injured, they exhibit much the same pain behavior as we do.

So, suppose we agree that animals feel pain. Should we care?

People concerned about animal suffering tend to focus on two broad areas: the use of animals for food and their use in scientific research. Let's address the latter area first.

Pharmaceutical products and medical procedures are routinely tested on animals before they are tested on human beings. These tests are designed to discover side effects, toxicity levels, and dangerous drug interactions. Out of necessity, these proce-

Jeremy Bentham (1748–1832) was an eccentric character. Legend has it that he directed that when he died his body should be donated to science, because that is where it would be most useful. However, he wanted it to be donated minus the head. It is rumored he believed science would one day figure out how to "restart" the brain. He wanted his head preserved so that he would be able to continue his useful contributions. Bentham's preserved skeleton, dressed in his own clothes, is still on display at University College of London, but a wax head is now in place of the real one. It is also rumored that he directed that his preserved head be placed on the table at the University's annual faculty meeting. This gives a new meaning to the phrase "head of the department"!

dures cause suffering and painful deaths. One of the most notorious cases involves the use of something called a "Noble-Collip Drum." Picture something like a large clothes dryer, with various metal bars attached to the inside. A creature is put inside and spun, so that the bars cause various kinds of external and internal injuries. This allows the researcher to test painkillers, or practice setting broken bones, or suturing lacerations. Critics of this practice argue that the same research be conducted in another way. What do you think?

Cosmetics and other commercial products are also often tested on animals. Two notorious tests are the Draize and LD50 tests. The Draize test is used for cosmetics, and is done on rabbits, because their eyes are quite similar to human eyes. The rabbits' eyes are pinned open, the product is pasted over the eye, and the results, usually quite painful for the rabbit, are observed. LD50 stands for Lethal Dose, 50%. It is a procedure to determine how much of a product it takes to kill half of the test population. For example, suppose you are testing bleach. You would take, say, 100 dogs, and continue forcing them to drink bleach until 50 of them die. Consider how many times you might have to run this experiment in order to get 50 to die.

Animal rights activists insist that Draize and LD50 are not needed. In fact, if you visit cosmetics counters at your local department store, you might be surprised to learn how many products now proudly bear the label "Not Animal Tested."

Concern for the welfare of animals seems to be on the rise. Most research and teaching institutions have some sort of Animal Care and Use committee, which enforces a policy designed to ensure the humane treatment of test subjects. They regulate things such as the animals' diet and the size of their cages.

These committees go a long way toward eliminating unnecessary suffering, but still do not do much to curtail the number of experiments performed. A stronger position is advocated by modern-day philosophers Tom Regan and Dale Jamieson, called the *limited use position.* According to this view, before being allowed to proceed with an experiment, the scientist must show that the potential benefit will realistically outweigh the harm to the subjects, and that there is no other reasonable way to obtain the knowledge. If the burden of proof is set quite high, this goes a long way toward eliminating unnecessary experimentation and suffering. We might also speculate that, because human beings can be quite ingenious when they are forced to be, scientists would soon come up with other ways of acquiring the knowledge they seek.

Some European countries ban experimentation on animals entirely. This may be too extreme, however. Very few of us would want to be the first mammal to ingest a new medication, or the first living creature to go under the surgeon's knife. The compromise position of Regan and Jamieson is a compromise between extremes.

Let's turn now to the use of animals for food. Here we must examine the position of Peter Singer (1946–), perhaps the best-known and most controversial moral philosopher alive today. In numerous articles and books, he argues for the moral significance of animals. Singer shares Bentham's moral philosophy of avoiding pain and pursuing happiness. He argues that we have a moral obligation to combat suffering wherever it is found, and in whatever species it is found. Moreover, Singer practices what he preaches: He is a vegetarian, and donates a high percentage of his salary and speaking fees to charity. He is not against subsistence hunting, only the cruel practice of factory farming.

Factory farming is the standard way of producing meat, poultry, and milk products today. A factory farm is a large industrial complex where animals are kept in extremely small cages and overfed for maximum profit. Singer is convinced that factory farming is not only cruel, but also inefficient. He argues that we could end world hunger if the land and energy needed to raise meat for human consumption were to be given over to crops such as rice and soy. For example, it is estimated that it takes roughly 283 gallons of oil in the form of fuel and fertilizer to produce one beef steer.

So far, we have focused mainly on mammals, and not much on other creatures. It is pretty clear we need not worry about the suffering of a bacterium, a mosquito, or an oyster. So, where do we draw the line? The answer, admittedly one that is not completely satisfying, is to admit that the dividing line is vague, and that there will be some hard cases in the middle. But, a vague boundary is still a boundary, and does not invalidate the fact that there are a lot of clear-cut cases.

Both Bentham and Singer subscribe to the results theory of ethics, so the question arises whether we have to agree with that philosophy in order to care about animals. The answer is no. Immanuel Kant's rule theory of ethics holds that human beings are required to do their duty regardless of the results. (For more on Kant's theory, known as *deontology*, see Chapter 6.) Kant denied that animals have rights on the grounds that rights require rationality, a property he thinks animals lack. Kant affirmed, however, that we have an indirect duty to prevent suffering in animals. He wrote,

> . . . our duties towards them (animals) are indirect duties to humanity. Since animals are an analogue of humanity, we observe duties to mankind when we observe them as analogues to this, and thus cultivate our duties to humanity. If a dog, for example, has served his master long and faithfully, that is an analogue of merit; hence I must reward it, and once the dog can serve no longer, must look after him to the end, for I thereby cultivate my duty to humanity, as I am called upon to do. . . . So if a man has his dog shot, because it can no longer earn a living for him, he is by no means in breach of any duty to the dog, since the latter is incapable of judgement [*sic*], but he thereby damages the kindly and humane qualities in himself, which he ought to exercise in virtue of his duties to mankind. Lest he extinguish such qualities, he must already practice a similar kindliness towards animals; for a person who already displays such cruelty to animals is also no less hardened towards men. We can already know the human heart, even in regard to animals. (From *Lectures on Ethics* by Immanuel Kant, 1775–1780/1997, p. 212)

Kant is telling us that respect for life in any form is something that all human beings should try to instill in themselves.

So, whether you side with Bentham and Singer or with Kant, you might be concerned about the treatment of animals in our society. When we look back in history and see how past generations mistreated women and people of color, we feel ashamed. Do you think future generations will look back at how we currently treat animals and feel ashamed of us? Many philosophers argue that our mistreatment of animals is one symptom of our disregard for the environment as a whole.

Discussion Questions

1. Review the dialogue at the beginning of this chapter. Would Nelson agree more with Bentham or Kant? What about Matt? Give evidence.
2. Name some living things you think feel pain. Name some you do not think feel pain.
3. Have you ever seen an animal mistreated? If so, how did it make you feel?
4. Do you know any vegetarians (people who don't eat meat)? Do you think Peter Singer is correct to suppose that if we all became vegetarians we could end world hunger?
5. Could you picture yourself working at a factory farm or at a laboratory that tests new products on animals? Why or why not?

Exercises

1. Write a dialogue between Janet and Jake. Janet argues that we have an obligation not to eat meat. Jake argues that that we do not.
2. Construct a thought experiment to test the claim that humans are superior to animals.

Activities

1. Draw a picture of your favorite animal. Try to convey in the picture why you like this animal.
2. Try living as a vegetarian for a week (no meat). If you're already a vegetarian, try being a lacto-ovo vegetarian (no meat, eggs, or dairy products). Create a Web log detailing your experiences.
3. Watch the movie *Babe* (1995), directed by Chris Noonan. Do you think it shows that animals have rights? Why or why not?
4. Visit a factory farm in your area and write an editorial for or against the continued use of factory farms to produce food supplies.

Community Action Steps

1. Volunteer at an animal shelter in your area.
2. Research the organization known as PETA (People for the Ethical Treatment of Animals). Do you agree or disagree with their mission. Write an essay supporting your viewpoints
3. Plan a meatless neighborhood picnic.

References

Bentham, J. (1970). *An introduction to the principles of morals and legislation* (J. H. Burns & H. L. A. Hart, Eds.). London: Athlone Press. (Original work published 1780)

Kant, I. (1997). *Lectures on ethics* (P. Heath, Trans.). Cambridge, England: Cambridge University Press. (Original works published 1775–1780)

Regan, T., & Jamieson, D. (1982). On the ethics of the use of animals in science. In T. Regan & D. VanDeVeer (Eds.), *And justice for all* (pp. 64–78). Lanham, MD: Rowman & Littlefield.

Singer, P. (2002). *Animal liberation.* New York: HarperCollins.

Further Reading

Bentham, J. (1970). *An introduction to the principles of morals and legislation* (J. H. Burns & H. L. A. Hart, Eds.). London: Athlone Press. (Original work published 1780)

Carlin, D. R. (2000, August). Rights: Animal and human. *First Things: A Monthly Journal of Religion and Public Life, 105,* 16–17.

DeGrazia, D. (2002). *Animal rights: A very short introduction.* Oxford, England: Oxford University Press.

Kant, I. (1956). *Groundwork for the metaphysic of morals* (H. J. Paton, Trans.). New York: Harper and Row. (Original work published 1785)

Kant, I. (1997). *Lectures on ethics* (P. Heath, Trans.). Cambridge, England: Cambridge University Press. (Original works published 1775–1780)

Regan, T., & Jamieson, D. (1982). On the ethics of the use of animals in science. In T. Regan & D. VanDeVeer (Eds.), *And justice for all* (pp. 64–78). Lanham, MD: Rowman & Littlefield.

Rollin, B. E. (2001, December 19). Farm factories: The end of animal husbandry. *The Christian Century, 118*, 26–29.

Singer, P. (1990). The significance of suffering. *Behavioral and Brain Sciences, 13*(1), 9–12.

Singer, P. (2002). *Animal liberation*. New York: HarperCollins.

Skidelsky, E. (2000, June 5). Nonsense on stilts. *New Statesman, 129*, 53–54.

Stephen, L. (1900). *The English utilitarians. Volume one: Jeremy Bentham*. London: Duckworth & Co.

CHAPTER 11
Who Will Take Care of the Environment?

The Car

Samantha runs into Tyrel at the bookstore. He is at the magazine rack browsing *Car and Driver* magazine. She walks up behind him and peeks over his shoulder.

SAMANTHA: I've never seen you with a car magazine. What's up?

TYREL: <*Startled at first, and then pleased to see her*.> Well, I need a new car. And, look at this Hummer. It's so cool! I'll be the biggest engine in the city.

SAMANTHA: <*Grimacing*> You shouldn't buy a thing like that. Think of how much gas it guzzles.

TYREL: <*Shrugging*> No problem, I can afford a few more gallons every week.

SAMANTHA: <*Punching him in the shoulder*> That's not the point. Think of how much pollution it produces. Most of us don't really need cars at all, and if you do need one, it should be one of these new gas/electric models that can get 60 miles per gallon instead of the nasty mileage a Hummer gets. We need to take better care of the planet.

TYREL: Samantha, it's a big planet! On such a large scale, the little bit of pollution I produce isn't going to make any noticeable difference.

SAMANTHA: But, what if everyone thought that way? There are billions of people in the world. If each one of us makes as much pollution as you, it's going to make a very noticeable difference. In order to keep the environment healthy and green, we all have to cut back and make sacrifices.

TYREL: I'm not choking to death yet, so the world is green enough for me.

SAMANTHA: But, what about your children? Don't you want your kids to have clean air and water?

TYREL: I'm not having kids, so as long as the air will still be breathable until I'm dead, I'm happy. I'm gonna look out for me.

SAMANTHA: Well, I think that's being selfish.

TYREL: Not at all. Being selfish is taking more than your fair share. I'm not taking more than anybody else. <*Pausing to think about what he just said.*> Or, at least no more than they would if they had the money.

SAMANTHA: Tyrel, we can all be happy taking so much less.

TYREL: Samantha, if you want to live in fear of the future, that's your business. But, if you want a ride in my car, you better change your tune!

Questions

- What is the definition of selfishness according to Samantha? What about Tyrel? Which definition do you agree with more?
- Do you think Tyrel is being selfish, or simply exercising his right to choose?
- Do you think the government should put a high "gas-guzzler" tax on Tyrel's dream car and others like it?
- Should recycling be mandatory? What sorts of things could you do to make a difference in helping to protect the environment?

Protecting the Environment

We are not being kind to Earth, our only home. The ozone layer that protects us from harmful solar rays is rapidly disintegrating. Air pollution in many cities is causing chronic health problems, and global warming threatens our coasts. (The next time you see a beautiful sunset, remember that much of the color you see is caused by smog particles in the air.) Overfishing and pollution threaten many species of fish with extinction. We are warned to limit consumption of certain kinds of fish because of the high levels of toxic pollutants they have ingested. The common practice of clear-cutting forests, or simply burning them down to make farmland, results in great numbers of plant and animal extinctions.

Some people maintain that we can find technological fixes for these problems, and therefore that we should not worry about them too much. Others insist that instead of hoping to fix problems we need to stop causing them. They worry that Earth's "disease" will advance so far that no amount of medicine will be able to cure the patient.

Early modern philosophers did not care much about the environment. The French philosopher René Descartes justified the mistreatment of animals by claiming they cannot feel pain. At the same time in England, Francis Bacon (1561–1626) argued that all of nature exists for us to use. He goes further, though, when he said that science will make nature a slave to man, in a way that does "not merely exert gentle guidance over nature's course, but having the power to conquer and subdue her, to shake her to her foundations" (from *Selected Philosophical Works*, by Francis Bacon, 1999, p. 506).

The same attitude is reflected throughout Bacon's culture. For example, the King James Bible, produced at roughly the same time, translates a passage in the book of Genesis as God granting man dominion over creation. The word *dominion* suggests power and control. More modern translations often use a word like *stewardship*, suggesting care and protection instead.

We have come a long way from Bacon's era. Today environmentalism is a fact of life. An *environmentalist* is someone who tries to conserve and recycle, rather than pollute and endanger nature. Although no one can avoid environmentalism in our society, each person chooses his or her own level of commitment to it.

Francis Bacon (1561–1626) was trained as a lawyer. Because his friend the Earl of Essex gave him an estate, he was reasonably wealthy. When the Earl was accused of treason, Bacon was named prosecutor, and he succeeded in getting his "friend" hanged! Although credited as the father of modern experimental science, Bacon was not much of an experimenter himself. He was more of a promoter, urging government funding for science. He did do one at least one experiment, however, and it caused his death. Living at a time before refrigeration, he wondered whether cold would help stop meat from rotting. One winter day he bought some chickens, packed some in snow and left some out in the air, and compared how quickly each would rot. Unfortunately, working in the cold and damp made him seriously ill, and he died shortly thereafter.

What personal sacrifices should we be prepared to accept? What sorts of reasons should motivate our commitment to environmentalism?

The terms *shallow ecology* and *deep ecology* capture two ends of the spectrum. Shallow ecology follows some of these ideas (Naess, 1998):

- Natural diversity is valuable as a resource for us.
- It is nonsense to talk about value except as value for mankind.
- Plant species should be saved because of their value as generic reserves for human agriculture and medicine.
- Pollution should be decreased if it threatens economic growth. (p. 138)

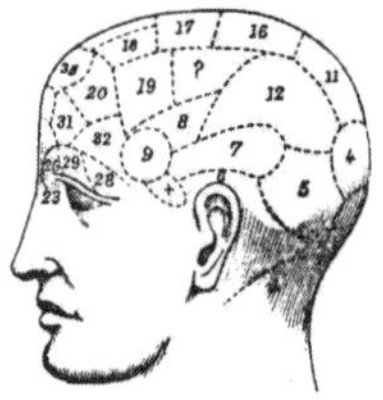

Thought Experiment:
The Grandchildren That Never Were

It is the year 2100. In the year 2090, World War III began. In the year 2095, a biological weapon that destroys the human immune system only was released and used by both sides in the war. As a result, human beings have become extinct. The beautiful parks that the people of the early 21st century worked so hard to build and protect are now enjoyed by no one but the squirrels and birds that live there. At the entrance of the biggest, most beautiful park of all, there is a golden plaque that reads as follows: *"This park is dedicated with love to our future grandchildren. We worked very hard and made many sacrifices, knowing that you would one day appreciate having this green space to enjoy."* Of course, the "future grandchildren" referred to in this plaque were never born, because their parents all died in WWIII. Was it still worth the effort? Should the people of the 21st century have put their effort toward preventing WWIII instead? Should we be thinking about our future grandchildren now?

We might think of shallow ecology as an extension of Bacon's view. It still views nature as a force to be harnessed and used for our purposes. We need to be environmentally conscious only in order to use it more effectively. We should keep our rivers, lakes, and oceans clean so our children and their children will have clean water to drink and swim in.

There are two troubling aspects to shallow ecology. The first is simply that it seems selfish to claim that nothing has value unless it has value to human beings. A second troubling aspect arises when we look beyond our existing family members. Why should we care about preserving the environment for them? How can these "possible people" have any value for you when they do not now—and may never—even exist?

Deep ecology is an attempt to respond to the troubling aspects of shallow ecology. It follows these ideas (Naess, 1998):

- Natural diversity has its own (intrinsic) value.

- Equating value with value for humans is nothing but prejudice.
- Plant species should be saved because of their intrinsic value.
- Decrease of pollution has priority over economic growth. (p. 138)

With its commitment to the intrinsic value of all forms of life, deep ecology solves the problems with shallow ecology, but it is also more demanding, as any unselfish act is bound to be.

The 20th-century philosopher Garrett Hardin (1915–2003) was a deep ecologist. In his view, we should treat the environment as valuable whether or not it is to our economic advantage. He writes,

> A number of years ago I decided to plant a redwood tree in my backyard. As I did so I mused, "What would my economist friends say to this? Would they approve? Or would they say I was an economic fool?"
>
> The seedling cost me $1.00. When mature the tree would (at the then current prices) have $14,000 worth of lumber in it—but it would take two thousand years to reach that value. Calculation showed that the investment of so large a sum of money as $1.00 to secure so distant a gain would be justified only if the going rate of interest was no more than 0.479 percent per year. So low a rate of interest has never been known. Plainly I was being a rather stupid "economic man" in planting that tree. <u>But I planted it.</u> (From "Who Cares for Posterity," by Garrett Hardin, 1998, p. 281)

Simply put, Hardin believes it costs more to pollute less. Clean landfills are difficult to site and expensive to build. Logging that preserves the forest is much less efficient than clear-cutting. Yet, Hardin is willing to put up with this cost. Why? Because he loves nature for its own sake. In the same way that we don't expect our friends to exist for our use, we should not expect nature to exist for our use.

Some philosophers believe that human beings are naturally selfish and that any philosophy that depends on unselfish acts is unrealistic. Others, however, insist that although human beings are often selfish, they do not have to be. In this chapter we have seen how there may be both selfish and unselfish reasons for caring about the environment.

Discussion Questions

1. Review the dialogue at the beginning of this chapter. Would Tyrel agree more with Bacon or Hardin? What about Samantha? Give evidence.
2. What do you think would be a fair sacrifice for the United States to make to protect the environment?
3. Would you be willing to pay a bit more for products you know are produced in an environmentally friendly way?
4. How might you respond to someone who says, "One person can never make a difference, so why should I bother?"
5. Do you regard nature as a tool or as a friend?

Exercises

1. Write a dialogue between Earl and Nancy. Earl argues that we have an obligation to recycle. Nancy argues that that we do not.
2. Construct a thought experiment to test the claim that technology can solve our environmental problems.

Activities

1. Draw a picture of your favorite place outdoors. Try to convey in the picture why you like it.

2. Visit a zoo or a botanical garden and compile a list of endangered species. What percentage of the zoo population is comprised of endangered species?

Community Action Steps

1. Write to your congressperson to urge better pollution control.
2. Set up a recycling program in your neighborhood.
3. Make and display posters showing the value of nature.

References

Bacon, F. (1999) *Selected philosophical works* (R. Sargent, Ed.). Indianapolis, IN: Hackett.

Hardin, G. (1998). Who cares for posterity? In L. Pojman (Ed.), *Environmental ethics* (pp. 279–284). New York: Wadsworth.

Naess, A. (1998). Ecosophy T: Deep versus shallow ecology. In L. Pojman (Ed.), *Environmental ethics* (pp. 137–144). New York: Wadsworth.

Further Reading

Bacon, F. (1999) *Selected philosophical works* (R. Sargent, Ed.). Indianapolis, IN: Hackett.

Hardin, G. (1998). Who cares for posterity? In L. Pojman (Ed.), *Environmental ethics* (pp. 279–284). New York: Wadsworth.

Huber, P. W. (1998, April). Saving the environment from the environmentalists. *Commentary, 105,* 25–31.

Madigan, T. J. (1993, Spring). On biodiversity: An exclusive interview with E. O. Wilson. *Free Inquiry, 13,* 12–18.

Naess, A. (1998). Ecosophy T: Deep versus shallow ecology. In L. Pojman (Ed.), *Environmental ethics* (pp. 137–144). New York: Wadsworth.

Wapner, P. (1996, May/June). Toward a meaningful ecological politics. *Tikkun, 11,* 21–26.

CHAPTER 12
What Would Happen if There Were No Governments?

The Protest

Dan has been unhappy since he learned that the city is going to stop subsidizing bus fare for needy students. He is joining a large number of his friends and neighbors in protest. They plan to form a picket line on the sidewalk in front of a major bus terminal asking no one to buy bus tickets until the subsidies are restored. When Dan arrives he hurries over to his friend, Jasmine.

DAN: <*Greeting Jasmine with a hug*> You look nervous. What's the matter?

JASMINE: <*Pulling away from him*> Well, to be honest, I'm having second thoughts about this protest. By blocking the sidewalk and making a public disturbance, we'll be costing the bus company and the businesses that depend on them a great deal of money. It seems hypocritical of us to rob them this way while protesting that they're robbing us.

DAN: But Jasmine, the Constitution of the United States recognizes the legitimacy of civil disobedience. We're breaking the law for a good reason! In fact, I don't think picketing will be enough. To attract the television reporters, we may have to break some windows. Come on! <*He starts to head off.*>

JASMINE: <*Shouting*> Wait a minute, Dan! The Constitution forbids violent demonstrations. If we damage any property or hurt anyone, then we show that we're just as inconsiderate as the city.

DAN: <*Turning back to face her*> Protesting has to be inconsiderate to be effective.

JASMINE: I disagree. I think we should write letters to the city council telling them all the reasons why we care about this bus subsidy.

DAN: <*Growing angry*> If you really cared, you'd take a braver stand. This is a serious matter. The livelihood of many people is on the line. People write letters just to feel good about themselves. I want results, and I want them now.

<Dan pulls a baseball bat out of his bag and stalks away, leaving Jasmine with her hand over her mouth.>

Questions

- How does Dan want to protest against the city? What about Jasmine? With whom do you agree more, and why?
- What do you think Martin Luther King, Jr. would do in this situation?
- Give an example of a time that you protested something you thought was unfair. Suppose somebody disagreed with you. How would you defend your actions?

Government

An *anarchist* is someone who advocates a society without any government. The word *anarchy* is often used informally for any unruly mob with a grudge. But, some philosophers defend anarchy as a legitimate political position. In 19th-century Russia there were many famous anarchists, including Leo Tolstoy, the author of *Anna Karenina* and *War and Peace*. Because the government in Russia at that time was one of the most repressive governments in history, it is not surprising that anarchism found a place to germinate there.

Given that anarchy is a serious possibility, we should ask what the justification for our own government is. We will address this question by looking at the theories of two early modern English political theorists, Thomas Hobbes and John Locke. We focus on these two not only because of their seminal influence on later political thought but also because each of them imagines what life would be like with no government at all.

Hobbes was a social contract theorist. *Social contract theory* holds that government is created and legitimized by an agreement among the citizens. This contract or agreement may not ever actually be written down or spoken. Most social contract theorists regard living in a country as a metaphorical way of signing a contract. If you take advantage of the benefits a government has to offer, then you are implicitly agreeing to live by its rules. The ancient philosopher Socrates is a good example of a social contract theorist. When he was arrested for corrupting the youth, his friends urged him to escape, but he refused on the grounds that it would be wrong to betray the government that had served and protected him his whole life.

Hobbes argued for social contract theory by asking us to imagine what life would be like without any government at all, in what philosophers call the *state of nature*. Hobbes viewed the state of nature as a perpetual war of everyone against everyone, where life is "solitary, poor, nasty, brutish, and short." (Hobbes, *Leviathan*, 1651/1975, p. 100). According to Hobbes, we make a contract with each other to have a government in order to escape the fear and chaos that is present in the state of nature. He wrote, "I authorize and give up my right of governing myself to this man . . . on this condition, that thou give up thy right to him, and authorize all his actions in a like manner" (Hobbes, *Leviathan*, 1651/1975, p. 132).

Thomas Hobbes (1588–1679) was fond of saying that he was born "a twin with fear," because his mother gave birth to him prematurely when she was frightened by the sound of the Spanish Armada arriving to do battle with England. Hobbes lived through the English Civil War, a very bloody period that included the execution of King Charles I. His book *Behemoth* is a history of the Civil War. The civil unrest Hobbes witnessed influenced his major political work, *Leviathan*, which presents a very harsh picture of human nature and the human condition. Even toward the end of a very long and productive life, he was still publishing. At the age of 84 he wrote his autobiography in Latin verse, and 2 years later he completed translations of Homer's *Iliad* and *Odyssey*.

John Locke (1632–1704) was an English philosopher whose writings influenced the framers of the Declaration of Independence and the United States Constitution. In contrast to Hobbes, in his later life, Locke lived in a time of peace and prosperity. Therefore, it is not surprising that his ideal form of government is less harsh and more respectful of human rights. He published important work on the nature of perception and of the self and human understanding. Politically, he was a strong advocate for the scientific study of nature. He also theorized on the nature of and justification for private property. On this topic, Locke is sometimes thought of as an early environmentalist because he suggested two rules governing private property: Take only as much as you need, and leave things in as good a shape, or better, than you found them.

Hobbes was convinced that human beings need a strong government to keep them from reverting to the state of nature. He therefore advocates absolute monarchy, where the citizens agree to give the king unlimited power. In this social contract, the people pledge complete obedience to the king in exchange for peace and security. To secure peace, the king can do anything he deems necessary (except harm the citizens). This means, for example, he could make it illegal for anyone to leave home after dark.

Why would we agree to such a harsh form of government? The answer, for Hobbes, is that the alternative is worse. If we opt out of the contract, we return to a state of war, and because there's no right or wrong in this anarchic state, we would probably not survive. As long as the king can protect us, we owe him our complete loyalty. Hobbes' theory is reflected throughout history: When people feel the threat of war, they are always more willing to accept limitations on freedom, even if those limitations aren't fair. In Hobbes's view, it is worth giving up freedom and equality for security.

John Locke (1632–1704) disagreed with Hobbes's concern for security. In his view, everyone has advantages and disadvantages in the state of nature. For example, you may be much stronger than your neighbors, but they may be richer than you. Locke insisted that, because our advantages and disadvantages tend to even out, the state of nature "is not a state of license" (Locke, 1689/1956, p. 5). In Locke's view, human beings are governed by a law of nature derived from reason, which says that we should not harm others or ourselves. This law of nature prevents us from falling into a perpetual war of everyone against everyone.

In Locke's vision of the state of nature, human beings use reason to live together in peace. So, what is the need for government? Human beings need government, in Locke's view, because we do not always act solely according to reason. When we or those close to us have a dispute—over property, for example—we become emotionally involved. Our emotions cloud our judgment and make it difficult for us to be impartial. We need government to settle disputes impartially for us.

Like Hobbes, Locke was a social contract theorist. He believed that we agree to give up some of our freedom in order to establish a ruler who can enforce an impartial system of punishment. According to Locke, however, this ruler should not have total power. Locke rejected the idea of an absolute monarchy because it leaves the citizens without the right of appeal. In an appeal, the citizens ask one judge to check the decision of another judge to make sure it is fair. A government with multiple powers that check and balance each other is more likely to stay impartial than a government with only one final judge.

Even though Locke lived under a monarchy, he was sympathetic to democracy. Already in his day the English monarchy had lost much of its power to an elected parliament. (Today, even though Great Britain has a queen, she has no real political power and her role is largely ceremonial.) Locke was also a minimalist about the role of government in our lives. In his view, the sole role of government is the protection of property. He would be critical of most democracies in existence today because they do so much more than protect property. For example, in the United States, the government provides food stamps for unemployed citizens. Do you think it would it be better or worse if the government did not do this?

Although the state of nature rarely erupts within a country, many philosophers see the relationship between countries as a state of nature. On the one hand, in a world troubled by war and terrorism, it is easy to see this relationship as hostile, as in Hobbes's theory. On the other hand, international bodies such as the United Nations suggest that countries are trying to cooperate and reason with one another, just as Locke envisioned. Which, if either, is the more accurate depiction of international relations in your view?

Thought Experiment:
An Island of Your Very Own

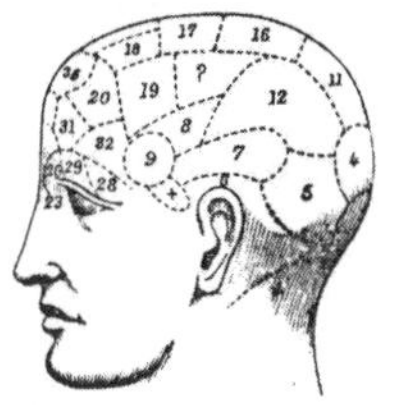

For your birthday this year, your best friend gives you a lottery ticket. "It may only have cost a dollar," he says, "but if you win, you will become the sole owner of a beautiful tropical island, along with 1 billion dollars to develop it as you see fit!" And, lucky for you, the ticket wins! As it turns out, the island is the size of Florida and has not been claimed by any country. So, suddenly, you are a king with a vast kingdom. As you set off for your island, you begin to think about what you will do with the billion dollars. How will you develop your island? Who else will you allow to live there? Will you need safeguards against possible violence and other forms of crime? Will you rule the island or will you let the inhabitants elect someone else to rule? What kind of rules would you like to see in place?

Discussion Questions

1. Review the dialogue at the beginning of this chapter. Would Dan agree more with Hobbes or Locke? What about Jasmine? Give evidence.
2. What is your view of human nature? Do you think that there is such a thing as human nature? Why or why not?
3. Name some examples of people giving up personal freedoms in a time of war. Can you think of an instance when this could become problematic?
4. Do you agree with Locke that the sole role of government should be the protection of property? Why or why not?
5. Do you agree with Hobbes that security is more important than freedom? Why or why not?

Exercises

1. Write a dialogue between Hunter and Lucie. Hunter argues that human beings would be better off without government. Lucie denies it.
2. Construct a thought experiment to test the claim that human beings are innately violent.

Activities

1. Look at the Declaration of Independence and the United States Constitution. Identify parts of those documents that you think sound Lockean, and which do not.
2. Watch the movie *Mad Max: Beyond Thunderdome* (1985), directed by George Miller. How does this movie envision the state of nature?
3. Observe legal proceedings at your local courthouse. Did you disagree with any of the trial's outcomes? Write a letter to the judge explaining your viewpoint.
4. Read *Lord of the Flies* by William Golding. Do you think Golding is suggesting that the state of nature is more like Hobbes' than it is like Locke's? How would you organize a society if you were one of the stranded boys?

5. Shadow a crime reporter for your local newspaper. Give a presentation to your class about what you observed.

Community Action Steps

1. Organize a protest regarding an issue that is important to you.
2. Invite a police officer or a judge to come to your school to talk about the law.
3. Volunteer to help register voters at election time.
4. Volunteer to work on a political campaign.

References

Hobbes, T. (1975). *Leviathan.* New York: Macmillan Publishing. (Original work published 1651)

Locke, J. (1956). *The second treatise of government* (T. P. Peardon, Ed.). New York: The Liberal Arts Press. (Original work published 1689)

For Further Reading

Hampton, J. (1997). *Political philosophy*. Boulder, CO: Westview Press.

Hobbes, T. (1975). *Leviathan.* New York: Macmillan Publishing. (Original work published 1651)

Klein, N. (2000, July 3). Does protest need a vision? *New Statesman, 129*, 23–25.

Locke, J. (1956). *The second treatise of government* (T. P. Peardon, Ed.). New York: The Liberal Arts Press. (Original work published 1689)

Nozick, R. (1974). *Anarchy, state, and utopia.* New York: Basic Books.

Rousseau, J. (1987) *Basic political writings* (D. Cress, Trans. & Ed.). Indianapolis, IN: Hackett.

PART 4

God

God the Father, 1682, Artus Quellin II

CHAPTER 13
Why Do Bad Things Happen to Good People?

The Saint

It is Friday night and Jake has a date with Hannah, but she doesn't show up. So, he goes to her house and finds her sitting on the back porch swing, staring vacantly off into space. It is clear that she has been crying.

JAKE: <*Approaching slowly, putting his hand on her shoulder*> What's the matter? Why so sad?

HANNAH: <*Snapping out of it with a start*> Oh Jake! We were supposed to meet at Jojo's tonight weren't we? I completely forgot! <*Apologetically*> My Aunt Minnie just called. Remember Blackie, the cute puppy she got after Uncle Bert died?

JAKE: <*Sitting down beside her*> Yeah.

HANNAH: Well, it just died from some sort of virus. Aunt Minnie is devastated.

JAKE: That's too bad. <*Pausing for a moment*> But, Hannah, she can get another dog.

HANNAH: <*Beginning to cry again*> But, she loved *that* one. It's all so unfair. Aunt Minnie is the nicest person who ever lived. She goes to church every Sunday, works tirelessly for charities even though she also has a full-time job, and she never holds a grudge against anyone. Everyone regards her as a saint, and yet bad things keep happening to her. Why did that virus have to kill her little Blackie?

JAKE: The virus didn't know she's a saint.

HANNAH: <*Getting angry*> But, God does! And, he could have stopped it.

JAKE: Maybe God was testing her faith.

HANNAH: Couldn't God find another way of testing her faith without killing a cute, innocent puppy? Anyway, if God knows everything, then he already knows her faith is strong. It makes me wonder whether God cares—whether he actually even exists!

JAKE: All I know is that when bad things happen to me, it makes me believe in God even more. I couldn't make it through the hard times without God. It's when I'm suffering that I feel his presence and the experience makes me a better person.

HANNAH: But, life doesn't always have a happy ending like that, Jake. For example, thousands of innocent people died in excruciating pain after that earthquake last year. Their suffering came to nothing but death. I don't think you'll see me in church again.

JAKE: Go slow girl. That's some pretty dangerous talk, what with your father being a Lutheran minister. Why don't you ask him about this?

HANNAH: Because I already know what he'll say, and it's the lamest thing you ever heard: "God works in mysterious ways."

Questions

- Why does suffering make Hannah doubt the existence of God? Why does it strengthen Jake's belief in God? Who do you agree with more and why?
- Describe something bad that happened to a good person you know. Do you think it happened for a reason? If so, what is the reason? If not, does this show that life is unfair? Explain.

Bad Things, Good People

There is a great deal of suffering in our world. Every day hundreds of small children finally die after wasting away from starvation. Every day thousands of women are brutally raped. Every day millions of people struggle endlessly with cancer and other debilitating diseases. Furthermore, when we watch the news, we see the horrific effects of natural disasters, environmental pollution, and war. It looks as though life on Earth is falling apart. If aliens from a distant galaxy visited our planet and observed the chaos in our lives they might wonder who is in charge. They might think our world is a giant mistake that is about to extinguish itself.

Many people believe that God is in charge and that he does not make mistakes. In their view, everything that happens, whether bad or good, happens for a reason. But, it is hard to understand how God could have a reason to let innocent people suffer. In the United States, if a mother lets her children starve, she will be declared an unfit guardian and the government will take her children away from her. Yet, if there is a God, he is letting his children starve day after day. Is there a way to reconcile the terrible pain in this world with the existence of God? This is known as the *problem of suffering.* Many philosophers disagree on this topic.

The 20th-century Australian philosopher J. L. Mackie (1917–1981) believed that the existence of so much suffering in the world indicates that God does not exist. This view is commonly known as *religious skepticism.*

Canvassing a wide variety of possible solutions to the problem of suffering, Mackie distinguished the "orthodox" ones from the "unorthodox" ones. Orthodox solutions preserve the traditional characteristics of God, while unorthodox solutions sacrifice one or more of them. God is traditionally characterized as all loving, all-powerful, and all knowing.

Mackie granted that it is relatively easy to come up with an unorthodox solution to the problem of suffering. For example, if God is angry and vengeful rather than all loving, then it would make sense that he would want to allow suffering in the world. Or, if God is all loving but not all-powerful, then, while he would not want to allow suffering, he might not be able to prevent it. Or, if God is not all knowing, then he might not be aware of how bad things have gotten down here on Earth. Each of these explanations could solve the problem of suffering.

John L. Mackie (1917–1981) was born in Sydney, Australia, and studied at the university there before going to Oriel College, Oxford. His teaching career has taken him to Sydney University, Otago University in New Zealand, and from 1967 until his death he was a Fellow of University College, Oxford. In 1974 he was made a Fellow of the British Academy. Mackie was a wide-ranging philosopher—in addition to his now classic work on the problem of evil, he has defended moral skepticism in *Ethics: Inventing Right and Wrong* (1977). As the title might suggest, defending moral skepticism is not the same as saying that there is no such thing as right and wrong. Mackie has written books on causation (*The Cement of the Universe* [1974]) and on paradox (*Truth, Probability, and Paradox* [1973]).

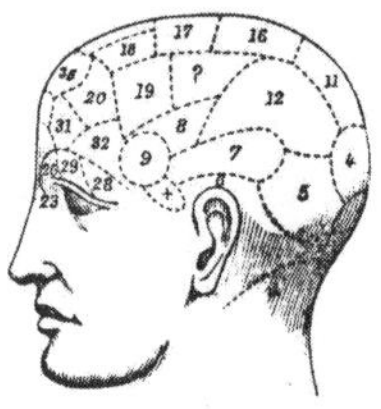

Thought Experiment:
The Next Dr. Frankenstein

Suppose you are going to make a monster out of body parts robbed from graves. For the monster's brain, you will use the brain of a dead criminal. Little did you know that this criminal's last thought before dying was his intention to kill his partner, Hans. Because this thought is still in the brain that you put into your monster, it is the first thought that the monster has when you bring him to life. So, naturally, the first thing your monster does is kills Hans. Are you responsible for Hans' death? Would it make a difference if you knew that this would happen? In this thought experiment you have brought a future killer to life. If God exists, he brings future killers to life every day. Is he responsible for the resulting deaths? Why or why not?

Few philosophers adopt unorthodox solutions like these, however, because once you give up the traditional characteristics of God, you don't really believe in God any more. Supernatural beings with flaws belong in comic book fiction, not in religion, these philosophers argue. True believers instead seek orthodox solutions.

The most widely held orthodox solution is known as the *freedom response*. In this view, suffering is the price we pay for having free will. Human beings cause suffering by making bad choices. So, God is not responsible, we are.

Mackie argued that there are two problems with the freedom response: First of all, it does not account for instances where humans suffer due to natural disasters. It's hard to explain something like an earthquake as a bad choice.

Secondly, Mackie argued that it is not at all clear why God could not have given us freedom along with the natural ability to make the right choices. Have you ever noticed how some people are lucky to be born with a natural ability? We all know someone like Ethan, who was born especially smart. He breezed through school without ever having to study and became a rocket scientist for NASA. Then there is Shanetta, who was born with an especially good nature. She never cried as a baby, never got in trouble growing up, and is now everyone's favorite nurse. Or, consider the real-life example of professional cyclist Lance Armstrong. He was born with extra-large lungs that make him so strong that he was able to win the world's most elite cycling race, the Tour de France, seven times. As examples like these show, God seems to be giving some people extra amounts of intelligence, kindness, or strength.

Now think about this for a moment: If God really is all-powerful, he could have made each and every one of us especially smart, kind, and strong altogether. Why not? There are no limits on his power. And, this would really improve our lives. So much suffering occurs when people behave in a stupid, unkind, or weak way. If

God eliminated—or at least reduced—the stupidity, unkindness, and weakness in human nature, the world would be a much better place. Someone might object that God cannot improve human nature without interfering with our freedom. In Mackie's view, however, this implies that God is not all-powerful, and therefore reveals that the freedom response is not an orthodox solution after all.

Mackie concluded that, although it is possible that God exists, the problem of suffering (which he calls "the problem of evil") proves that it is more likely that God does not exist. Mackie wrote:

> I can only state my convictions that there is no cogent positive argument for the existence of God, that the problem of evil constitutes an insuperable difficulty for any orthodox theism, that the advance of scientific knowledge renders a theistic view . . . superfluous as an explanatory hypothesis and utterly implausible, and that no specific revelation—such as would be needed to make the proposed view morally significant—has reliable credentials. (From *Ethics: Inventing Right and Wrong*, 1979, p. 232)

For Mackie, religion just does not make sense.

In contrast to Mackie, the medieval Roman philosopher St. Augustine of Hippo (354–430) presents a *theodicy*, which means "justification of God." It provides a solution to the problem of suffering. Although Augustine developed his theodicy 1,600 years ago, many people today still think it is the best answer to religious skepticism.

Augustine based his theodicy on his own life experience. He had a happy and carefree childhood because he grew up in the Roman Empire during a time of success and prosperity. By the time he reached adulthood, however, the Roman Empire began falling into a deep and rapid decline. Before long, fierce Germanic tribes invaded Rome, called the "eternal city," and burned it to the ground. Life soon became so terrible and desperate that everyone thought the world was coming to an end.

This sudden transition from success and prosperity to terrible desperation made Augustine realize how fragile and temporary this world is. He began to see life on Earth as nothing but a brief journey on the way to heaven. Any happiness that we may think we experience in this life is really nothing compared to the hap-

In addition to being a philosopher, Saint Augustine (354–430) was a very important bishop in the Catholic Church. Augustine wrote about his personal life in a book called *Confessions*, which is considered the first autobiography ever written. In it, he tells the famous story of the pear tree. When he was a child, he and some friends snuck into a neighbor's yard and climbed a pear tree. The tree was full of beautiful, ripe pears that would be valuable on the market. But, the boys made a game of snatching all the pears off the tree and tossing them into the pigsty. Reflecting on this incident in *Confessions*, Augustine expresses a great deal of shame and remorse. He asserts that the incident shows that there is evil in the human heart, even in children. Do you agree?

piness that the next life has to offer. In fact, it is foolish to try to enjoy success and prosperity in this world, Augustine asserted, because this only distracts us from our true purpose, which is to love God. God allows us to suffer in this life to purify us and prepare us for heaven, where we will live free of distraction and suffering for all eternity. Augustine wrote that

> our human life, though it is compelled by all the great evils of this age to be wretched, is happy in the expectation of a future life in so far as it enjoys the expectation of salvation too. For how can a life be happy, if it has no salvation yet? . . . As therefore, we are saved by hope, so it is by hope that we have been made happy; and as we have no hold on a present salvation, but look for salvation in the future, so we look forward to happiness, and a happiness to be won by endurance. For we are among evils, which we ought patiently to endure until we arrive among those goods where nothing will be lacking to provide us ineffable delight, nor will there be anything that we are obliged to endure. (From *The City of God Against the Pagans*, 413–426/1960–1966, Vol. iii, p. 535)

For Augustine, although there is no salvation from suffering in this life, the next life, with God in heaven, will make it all worthwhile.

Discussion Questions

1. Review the dialogue at the beginning of this chapter. Would Hannah agree more with Mackie or with Augustine? What about Jake? Give evidence.
2. Do you find any of the unorthodox solutions to the problem of evil attractive? Why or why not?
3. Do you agree with Mackie that one can possess free will without ever choosing wrongly? Why or why not?
4. Do you agree with Augustine that our only true happiness in this life lies in hope for a future life? Explain your view.

Exercises

1. Write a dialogue between Hannah and her father, the Lutheran minister, which continues the debate on the problem of suffering from where it left off in the opening dialogue.
2. Construct a thought experiment to test the claim that suffering makes you stronger.

Activities

1. Watch the movie *Time Bandits* (1981), directed by Terry Gilliam. Do you think humor is a good way to deal with the problem of suffering?
2. Listen to the song "Dear God" by XTC. What do you think it is trying to say?
3. Interview a local priest or minister about the problem of suffering. Write a speech providing solutions to the problem.
4. Watch the news and make list of the suffering around the world. Create a Web site detailing issues of suffering around the world.

Community Action

1. Join an organization devoted to feeding the hungry. Participate in food drives and soup kitchens in your community.
2. Volunteer as an activity coordinator in the terminal cancer ward at a hospital.
3. Investigate the Lance Armstrong Livestrong Foundation. If you agree with their mission, offer to volunteer for the organization's campaign.
4. Identify a friend or family member who is suffering and do something to help.

References

Augustine. (1960–1966). *The city of God against the pagans* (W. M. Green, Trans.). Cambridge, MA: Harvard University Press. (Original work written 413–426)

Mackie, J. L. (1979). *Ethics: Inventing right and wrong.* New York: Pelican Books.

Mackie, J. L. (1990). Evil and omnipotence. In M. Adams & R. Adams (Eds.), *The problem of evil.* Oxford, England: Oxford University Press. (Original work published 1955)

For Further Reading

Augustine. (1960–1966). *The city of God against the pagans* (W. M. Green, Trans.). Cambridge, MA: Harvard University Press. (Original work written 413–426)

Augustine. (1993). *Confessions* (F. J. Sheed, Trans.). Indianapolis, IN: Hackett. (Original work written 397–398)

Kaye, S., & Thomson, P. (2001). *On Augustine.* Belmont, CA: Wadsworth.

Mackie, J. L. (1979). *Ethics: Inventing right and wrong.* New York: Pelican Books.

Mackie, J. L. (1990). Evil and omnipotence. In M. Adams & R. Adams (Eds.), *The problem of evil.* Oxford, England: Oxford University Press. (Original work published 1955)

Planatinga, A. (1970). *The problem of evil.* Grand Rapids, MI: Eerdmans.

CHAPTER 14
What Is the Meaning of Life?

The Real You

Hallie and Markita are sisters. They have always been close, but they have not seen each other much over the past year, ever since Hallie went to live with their father. They are driving home, having just spent the day shopping together.

MARKITA: You seem different now. <*Markita looks at her sister.*> Not in a bad way, I guess. It's just that I feel like you're not the same person I used to know.

HALLIE: <*Surprised*> What do you mean, "different"?

MARKITA: Well, you're into different music, different foods, and different TV shows. . . . I guess it's that new boyfriend of yours.

HALLIE: Uh huh, P. J. <*Grinning*> I feel like he's helping me discover who I really am.

MARKITA: What do you mean, "discover who you really are"? How is the new you any more real than the old you?

HALLIE: <*Hallie pauses for a moment.*> I think each person is born with a soul, buried deep inside. Life is all about trying to get in touch with it. I feel like I'm getting closer.

MARKITA: <*Markita frowns.*> If you'd have hooked up with some other, completely different boy instead, you'd be feeling it with him!

HALLIE: Come on, Markita. <*Hallie laughs.*> You've changed, too.

MARKITA: Maybe so. But, at least I realize I'm creating myself as I go. I think we're all born blank, like an empty computer disk. Who you become depends on what you save on the disk. Any kind of music, food, TV, or boyfriend can become part of me if I want. That's why I'm careful how I pick and choose.

HALLIE: Well, I'm careful, too! I'm careful because I want to fulfill my destiny. I find out each day a little bit more about what my destiny is. You don't even think you have a destiny. <*Hallie rolls her eyes.*> You think life is all about making it up as you go along.

MARKITA: That's right. I see my life as an invention—and what's so bad about that? I'd rather make it up as I go along than play some role in a movie written by somebody else.

HALLIE: It's a great role in a great movie.

MARKITA: It's still just a role.

HALLIE: <*Dejected*> Wow, I never realized we saw life so differently.

MARKITA: <*Whispering*> Me either.

HALLIE: <*Hallie smiles.*> But, I guess talking wouldn't be any fun if everybody saw everything the same way.

MARKITA: That's true. We should talk more often.

Questions

- What is life all about according to Hallie? What is it all about according to Markita? With whom do you agree more, and why?
- Describe a change you've noticed in yourself lately. Do you think you discovered it buried deep in you all along or do you think you invented it? How could you prove it?

The Meaning of Life

Philosophers are famous for asking "What is the meaning of life?" It's a question we should all ask ourselves from time to time. The problem is, not only are there a lot of different answers to the question, there are a lot of different ways of understanding the question itself. One way of understanding the question is depicted in the opening dialogue. Do you discover the real you or do you create the real you? Your answer to this question will depend a lot on whether you are a theist, an atheist, or an agnostic.

Agnostics are people who believe that we can never attain adequate answers to profound questions such as the existence of God or the meaning of life. Because these profound questions cannot be settled in the same manner as scientific questions, such as the existence of distant planets or the cause of a disease, agnostics therefore recommend that we suspend judgment on these issues. Some philosophers have pointed out, however, that agnosticism may not be a coherent position because we have to make a decision one way or another, and because we cannot help but display our true answer in how we live our lives.

Theists are those who believe in the existence of an almighty God (or gods) who created the world. Most theists hold that God has a plan for creation. Because humans play an important part in this plan, theists are likely to assert that God has a plan for each and every one of us, a destiny. As we go through life we find out what our destiny is.

It would not make much sense for God to destine Julio to become a great scientist unless he created Julio with an innate ability and interest in science. Likewise, Emily cannot fulfill her destiny as an artist without a natural talent for art. So, it seems that if God has a plan for us, then he built us with this plan in mind, and it would be a good idea to start figuring out how we are built so that we can proceed accordingly.

Thomas Aquinas (1225–1274) is one of the most famous theist philosophers. He made an important distinction between essence and existence. Your *essence* is what you really are deep down inside. Your *existence* is what you do throughout your life. Aquinas argued that your essence existed in God's mind long before you were ever born. As you go through your life you make choices that change your *existence*, but you cannot change your *essence*, because it's your true nature and it determines the ultimate form that your life must take.

St. Thomas Aquinas (1225–1274) was a medieval Italian philosopher and Dominican priest. He is famously illustrated with the church in one hand and Aristotle's writings in the other, because he was a follower of Aristotle and wanted to make Aristotle's ideas consistent with Catholicism. Although his views were attacked from many quarters during his lifetime (at one point he had to give up his teaching post), they would soon come to dominate Catholic philosophy. He was made a saint in 1323, and pronounced an "Angelic Doctor" in 1567). Aquinas' greatest work is his *Summary of Theology* or *Summa Theologica*, which is an encyclopedia of arguments concerning every aspect of his faith. Just before he died, Aquinas had a mystical experience that convinced him that his life's work was worthless. Can you reconcile this with his view about destiny?

According to Aquinas, God is the creator of the universe because he alone is able to put essences into existence. In so doing, he makes something out of nothing. Putting an essence into existence is what it is to create a being. Aquinas wrote,

> It sufficiently appears at the first glance, according to what precedes, that to create can be the action of God alone. For the more universal effects must be reduced to the more universal and prior causes. Now among all effects the most universal is being itself: and hence it must be the proper effect of the first and most universal cause, and that is God. . . . Now to produce being absolutely, not as this or that being, belongs to creation. Hence it is manifest that creation is the proper act of God alone. (From *Summa Theologica*, by Thomas Aquinas, 1265–1272/1920, Question 45, Article 5).

Humans can "produce being" by taking something that already exists and making it into this or that, relatively speaking. For example, we could take a tree and make it into a table or a chair. In doing so, we never change its essence. Likewise, you might choose to be a doctor or a lawyer, thereby changing something that already exists into this or that. But, you cannot create your own being or who you really are.

Atheists are those who assert that there is no such thing as God. They hold that God is an idea like Santa Claus that societies around the world have popularized in order to prevent misbehavior, or because they lacked the scientific sophistication to understand the world around them. Because there is no divine creator in this viewpoint, there is no ultimate plan for human beings, and therefore no individual destiny. As we go through life we create ourselves.

Atheists don't deny that human beings are built with natural talents and traits. But, they do deny that these talents and traits are God-given. Therefore, you shouldn't interpret them as a sign of what you are supposed to do with your life. You may be born with scientific ability, but you may decide to invent yourself as an artist instead. Because agnostics claim that we cannot know whether there is a God, their attitude toward the question of human purpose typically resembles that of the atheist.

Jean-Paul Sartre (1905–1980) is one of the most famous atheist philosophers. He was also an existentialist. *Existentialism* is the view that free choice is the defining characteristic of human existence. Existentialism is popular among atheists, although it is possible for theists to be existentialists, too. In fact, in his work called *Existentialism is a Humanism*, Sartre argues that theists must be existentialists because belief in God is not like believing in the planets, which is something that can be settled by science. Rather, belief is God requires a leap of faith, which is an act of the will. The 19th-century Danish philosopher Søren Kierkegaard (1813–1855) is considered the first Christian existentialist. Insisting that God is the only thing that can make human life meaningful, he wrote, "If a human being did not have an eternal consciousness, if underlying everything there were only a wild, fermenting power . . . what would life be then but despair?" (From *Kierkegaard's Writings, Vol. VI*, by Søren Kierkegaard, 1983, p. 15)

Sartre did not agree, however, that God is needed to make human life meaningful. He turned Aquinas's distinction between existence and essence upside down. While Aquinas asserted that human essence precedes human existence, Sartre asserted that human existence precedes human essence. Sartre wrote,

> What is meant here by saying that existence precedes essence? It means that, first of all, man exists, turns up, appears on the scene, and, only afterwards, defines himself. If man, as the existentialist conceives him, is indefinable, it is because at first he is nothing. Only afterward will he be something, and he himself will have made what he will be. Thus there is no human nature, since there is no God to conceive it. Not only is man what he conceives himself to be, but he is also only what he wills himself to be after this thrust toward existence. (From *Existentialism and Human Emotions*, by Jean-Paul Sartre, 1957, p. 15)

Sartre held that self-creation is what makes human beings responsible for the way they live their lives. He was critical of the theistic belief in destiny because he believed that this enables people to make excuses for themselves, such as, "I guess it was my destiny to become a secretary, rather than a great writer." According to Sartre, it's beneath the dignity of a human being to believe that there's nothing you can do about who you are. He called this belief *bad faith*.

A nihilist is someone who does not believe that life is meaningful at all. (The term *nihilist* comes from the Latin word *nihil*,

Jean-Paul Sartre (1905–1980) was a 20th-century French philosopher. He is well known for his friendship with a woman named Simone de Beauvoir (1908–1986). de Beauvoir was a philosopher, too, even though it was very rare for women to be philosophers until the end of the 20th century. She and Sartre agreed about many things and each inspired many of the other's works. They deny the existence of any human essence, insisting instead that we are what we make ourselves to be. For example, de Beauvoir claims that if you are a genius, it is because you became one on your own; you were not born a genius. de Beauvoir (1953) also went so far as to say, "One is not born a woman, one becomes one" (p. 267). What do you think she meant?

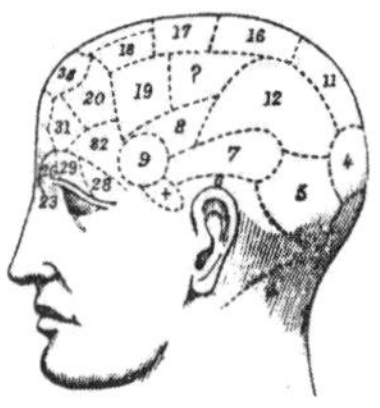

Thought Experiment:
The Most Important Choice of All

Suppose there is a genie with the power to turn time back to before you were born. She gives you the opportunity to decide who you want to be. Would you choose to be you? If so, does this show that you have a healthy self-esteem, or does it show that you think too highly of yourself? Suppose you have to choose to be somebody or something else. Who or what would you choose to be and why? In the *Republic*, Plato raises the question of reincarnation, the view that when you die you are reborn again as someone or something else. When he asks one hero of Greek mythology, Odysseus, what he would like to be in his next life, Odysseus replies that he would like to be a swan. Plato praises Odysseus' choice, while criticizing people who choose to be rich, or famous, or powerful. Why do you suppose Odysseus chooses to be a swan, and why do you think Plato criticizes the other choices?

meaning "nothing.") Both Aquinas and Sartre reject nihilism, but in different ways.

For Aquinas, life has *objective value.* This is to say that our existence is important and has a purpose independently of how we feel about it. It's easy to see what Aquinas means in the case of a doctor who discovers a cure for cancer: The doctor's contribution to human good has an objective value. But, Aquinas holds that the same value applies to less-accomplished individuals. Suppose you're arrested at a very young age and spend your entire life in prison. Regardless of whether you know it or not, you're still fulfilling your destiny.

According to Sartre, in contrast, life has *subjective value.* We have to impose meaning on our existence in order for it to have purpose and importance. We do this by making commitments and working on projects that we find satisfying. Suppose you decide to spend your entire life counting blades of grass in a field. This can be a meaningful life if you find it satisfying. On the other hand, suppose you devote your life to healing the sick and have much success, but you do not find it satisfying. This would then be a meaningless life in Sartre's view. For him, what is important is how you feel about it.

In this final chapter, we have looked at some possible ways of addressing the question, "What is the meaning of life?" There are many others. The world we live in contains many different kinds of people with many different ways of seeing things. Philosophy helps us understand and appreciate these differences. Because of this, philosophy is one of the best ways of making life meaningful. We hope that you continue your search for morality, beauty, truth, justice, and meaning in your life.

Discussion Questions

1. Review the dialogue at the beginning of this chapter. Would Markita agree more with Aquinas or Sartre? What about Hallie? Give evidence.
2. Give an example of a change you have made that either reveals who you really are or shows what you want to be.
3. If you were going to write a best-selling autobiography, what would you call it? Why?
4. Do you agree with Sartre that it is beneath the dignity of a human being to believe that there's nothing you can do about who you are?
5. Do you think that Sartre is correct when he argues that theists must be existentialists because belief is a matter of will?

Exercises

1. Write a dialogue between Gigi and Ishubu. Gigi contends that she cannot become an artist because she has no artistic ability. Ishubu contends that she can.
2. Construct a thought experiment to test the claim that free choice is the defining characteristic of human existence.

Activities

1. Watch the movie, *Monty Python's The Meaning of Life* (1983), directed by Terry Gilliam and Terry Jones. Is there an argument in the humor?
2. Start a record of your dreams. What do they tell you about who you are or who you want to be?
3. Write a letter to yourself describing who you want to be in 1 year and arrange for someone to mail it to you in 1 year.
4. Watch three different biography programs on TV or video and write an essay, discussing whether they prove that essence precedes existence or the other way around.
5. Write an autobiographical story that reveals who you really are.

Community Action Steps

1. Write a letter to a friend explaining who you think they really are.
2. Throw a party and ask everyone to bring the movie, the book, and the song that most expresses who they really are.
3. Get together with your family members and choose a symbol that best represents your family.

References

Aquinas, T. (1920). *Summa theologica* (2nd ed., Fathers of the English Dominican Province, Trans.). Retrieved December 12, 2005, from http://www.newadvent.org/summa/104505.htm (Original work written 1265–1272)

de Beauvoir, S. (1953). *The second sex* (H. M. Parshley, Trans.). New York: Alfred A. Knopf.

Kierkegaard, S. A. (1983). *Kierkegaard's writings: Vol. VI* (H. V. Hong & E. H. Hong, Trans. & Eds.). Princeton, NJ: Princeton University Press.

Sartre, J. (1957). *Existentialism and human emotions.* New York: Philosophical Library.

For Further Reading

Aquinas, T. (1920). *Summa theologica* (2nd ed., Fathers of the English Dominican Province, Trans.). Retrieved December 12, 2005, from http://www.newadvent.org/summa/104505.htm (Original work written 1265–1272)

Bretall, R. (Ed.). (1973). *A Kierkegaard anthology.* Princeton, NJ: Princeton University Press.

de Beauvoir, S. (1953). *The second sex* (H. M. Parshley, Trans.). New York: Alfred A. Knopf.

Inglis, J. (2002). *On Aquinas.* Belmont, CA: Wadsworth.

Kamber, R. (2000). *On Sartre.* Belmont, CA: Wadsworth.

Kierkegaard, S. A. (1983). *Kierkegaard's writings: Vol. VI* (H. V. Hong & E. H. Hong, Trans. & Eds.). Princeton, NJ: Princeton University Press.

Palmer, D. (2000). *Visions of human nature: An introduction.* Columbus, OH: Mayfield.
Sartre, J. (1957). *Existentialism and human emotions.* New York: Philosophical Library.
Scholz, S. J. (2000). *On de Beauvoir.* Belmont, CA: Wadsworth.
Taylor, R. (2004). The meaning of life. In D. Benatar (Ed.), *Life, death, and meaning: Key philosophical readings on the big questions* (pp. 19–28). Lanham, MD: Rowman & Littlefield.

APPENDIX A

Dialogue Worksheet

Date: ______________________

Group Name: ____

Dialogue Length: ____

Dialogue Title: ____

Writer: ____

Director: ____

Narrator: ____

Actors: (1) ____

(2) ____

(3) ____

(4) ____

(5) ____

Philosophical Question Raised by Dialogue: ________________________

____

Comments/Feedback (to be filled out after performance): ______________

____

____

____

DIALOGUE OUTLINE

The Setting: ______________________________

The Action: ______________________________

The Point: ______________________________

APPENDIX B
The Trial and Death of Socrates, and Plato's Theory of Forms

(For use with Chapter 1)

Socrates is philosophy's martyr. He was put to death in 399 B.C. for simply doing philosophy; that is, for publicly and critically examining the opinions held by powerful and famous people. Indeed, Plato's student Aristotle had to leave Athens when his philosophizing got him into trouble. He is reported to have said that he was leaving to prevent the Athenians from sinning twice against philosophy, Socrates being their first victim. In this appendix we will look at Socrates' life, trial, conviction, and death sentence. We will also look at Plato's most famous theory, his *theory of forms*.

Most people who read Plato start with the three dialogues that chronicle the trial and death of Socrates. These are *Apology*, *Crito*, and *Phaedo*. *Apology* is the Greek word for defense, and in this piece he defends himself against the charges that he corrupted the youth and did not believe in the official gods of the city. (Think about the way we use the word *apology* today. To what extent do you think that saying "I'm sorry" is a kind of defense?) Crito is the name of a friend of Socrates who visits him in jail as Socrates awaits his execution, and they discuss whether it is OK to break bad laws. *Phaedo* is a record of a conversation that takes place the night before Socrates is executed. This dialogue concerns what happens after death, and questions such as: Do we have a soul? If so, what happens to it after our bodies die? The dialogue ends with Socrates' dying by drinking hemlock (the Greek equivalent of lethal injection). So, what got Socrates into such trouble? Let's go back in time a bit and look at his life.

The city-state of Athens in which Socrates lived his entire life was the Western world's first democracy. It wasn't a democracy like any practiced around the world today. For instance, women could not vote. Also, slavery was legal then, and slaves could not vote. And, it was not a representative democracy. Instead, all of the citizens would gather in one place for debate, voting, and trials (some 501 citizens acted as jurors in Socrates' trial). The birth of democracy brought with it the need for a new set of skills: the power of persuasion and the answers to questions such as "What is justice?," "What is the best system of education?," and "What is a good life?" In a dictatorship, the answer to "What is justice?" is whatever the dictator says. But, in a democracy, "might" does not make "right." Thus, there arose a class of people called *sophists*, who claimed to be able to answer these questions, for a fee of course. The word *sophist* comes from the Greek word *sophia*, which means wisdom. But, look it up in a contemporary dictionary and you will see that it now has a pejorative tone; it refers to someone who makes an argument that sounds good, but is flawed in some important way.

What Socrates did to the sophists on the streets of Athens might have had something to do with this shift in meaning. What Socrates did was expose many of these sophists as frauds. But, what is important here is the way Socrates approached the claims of the sophists. If a sophist claimed to know, for example, that justice should be defined as "telling the truth and paying your debts," Socrates would not offer an alternative definition and claim it was better. Rather, he would ask a series of questions to tease out the implications of the sophist's definition. Making one's partner in conversation reason out the implications of her position, and actually doing the learning instead of listening to a lecture, is called the Socratic Method. Have you noticed that your best teachers will not just tell you the answer, but will make you figure it out? Do you find that you remember things better because of this?

Here is a very simple example of the Socratic Method in action: Sticking with the example of the definition of justice defined by a sophist as telling the truth and repaying debts, a modern day Socrates might simply ask whether justice demanded that one tell the truth to a 4-year-old about the existence of Santa Claus. (Have a look at Chapter 10 for a more sophisticated example of when lying might be the right thing to do and not be unjust.) As for justice demanding that we must always repay our debts, Socrates sets up a scenario similar to this:

> Suppose someone lends you a deadly weapon. According to your definition of justice you have to give it back when that person asks for it. But, suppose that when he

> asks for it he is in a mad rage at someone close to him, and you know that if you give the weapon back to him, in his crazed state he will do this other person harm, something he will regret tomorrow. Does justice really demand that you repay this debt to him?

So, what the Socratic Method has demonstrated here is that the sophist doesn't really know what justice is, and one of two things can happen now: The sophist can admit defeat, or, as Socrates would prefer, the conversation can continue and the two can attempt to improve on the definition of justice. In either case, though, the sophist has been exposed. (See Plato's *Republic* at http://www.litrix.com/republic/repub001.htm, for more on this idea.)

Now, if you can imagine Socrates doing this throughout a long life, with every sophist in town and at every meeting of the citizens, then you can understand why he made some powerful enemies. People also accused Socrates of being a sophist. In fact, he is parodied in a play called *The Clouds*, by Aristophanes, in which we are introduced to a Socrates who literally has his head in the clouds as he runs a school to help people make the weaker argument appear stronger. But, Socrates wasn't a sophist for two reasons. First, he took no money for his wisdom; he was a sculptor by trade. Second, in what is probably the second most quoted remark in *Apology* (after "The unexamined life is not worth living"), he says that if anything makes him wise, it is his not claiming to know what he does not know. We all can probably think of examples of people who think they know what they are talking about, but really don't. And, isn't Socrates right when he says that these people are much more foolish than those who simply admit that they don't know the answer to something?

So, this is why we find Socrates on trial for his life in *Apology*. He defends himself, but the jury had its mind made up before the trial begins, and he is found guilty. Then there is the Athenian version of a plea bargain to decide his sentence. The prosecutor and the defendant each propose a sentence, and the jury picks one. The prosecutor proposes the death sentence. Socrates' friends urge him to propose a small fine, which they could easily pay and would let the accusers save face. But, Socrates proposes that the city should pay him to keep doing what he does! He argues that his whole defense has been that his questionings only benefit the city, and that if the jury really thinks he is doing harm then they should sentence him to death. Is Socrates sincere, or is this just a big bluff? Read *Apology* and decide for yourself. If Socrates' proposed penalty is a bluff, it did not work, for Socrates is sentenced to death.

Quite a few days lie between the sentencing and the scheduled execution, and not surprisingly, many Athenians begin to have second thoughts. Think about people who have died in the service of a cause—people such as Martin Luther King, Jr., Abraham Lincoln, Mahatma Gandhi, and Jesus Christ. The deaths themselves may be tragic, but think about what these deaths do to advance the cause. The Athenians are rightly worried that Socrates' execution will serve as a rallying cry for Socrates' followers and for philosophy (which is exactly what happens). So, they make it clear that they wouldn't mind if Socrates were to escape and go into exile. But, when his friend Crito visits Socrates in prison to propose this, Socrates, always the philosopher, pauses to ask whether it would be the ethical thing to do. And, he concludes that he must accept his punishment, even though he doesn't believe that he has done anything wrong. He argues that if we willingly choose to live under the rule of law in a particular country, this constitutes a kind of contract to obey the laws, even those we don't like. We either have to follow legal means to change such laws or accept them. Socrates argues that as long as due process is followed, he must accept his punishment. Compare this with some of the other people mentioned above. Gandhi and Martin Luther King, Jr., for example, argue that *civil disobedience* (nonviolent protest) is sometimes necessary to change bad laws.

This brings us to the dialogue *Phaedo*, and the conversation that takes place the night before Socrates dies. As we mentioned earlier, the topic of the conversation is whether the soul survives the death of the body. (Try not to think of "soul" in any religious way. Think of it as whatever it is that makes you who you are—your personality, beliefs, memories, or feelings.) Now, the argument is too long and complicated to review here, but we will look at how Plato introduces his *theory of forms* in this dialogue about Socrates.

Recall that forms are *abstract ideas*. The Greek word for form is *eidos*, the root of our word *idea*. Today in Greece, you are most likely to find the word *eidos* on the menu of a pizza shop, referring to the kind of pizza you want. So, let's try to put these thoughts together in an example. Think of a stop sign. It is a red octagon. But, an octagon isn't red, and it isn't any particular size, it is a kind of geometric shape. Moreover, you won't find any perfect octagons in this world; nothing will exactly fit the definition—the lines won't be quite straight, the angles not quite sharp, and every physical octagon is a particular size, while the definition applies to all sizes. So, it makes sense to think that these abstract ideas are somehow different from their physical manifestations. Mathematicians who believe that these abstract ideas of shape and number are real and in a realm that somehow transcends the physical world are called Platonists. Plato himself went much further and asserted that the world of ideas contained much more than mathematical ideas, but also, as we noted in Chapter 1, the true causes for things being beautiful, or just, or good.

The Allegory of the Cave

At the beginning of Book VII of his book *Republic*, Plato has his character Socrates tell a story that is meant to clarify the theory of forms. We are to imagine a group of prisoners chained facing the wall of the cave, with the cave entrance and a fire behind them. They cannot turn their heads. Other people take turns walking behind them with puppets, so the prisoners see and hear a "shadow play." Socrates says that the prisoners would talk about the shadows as if they were the real thing, and need never learn that they are mistaken. We are to imagine next that a prisoner is unchained and taken into bright sunlight. At first he would be blinded, and want to return to the cave. But, as his eyes grow accustomed to the light he will recognize the real objects that were the cause of the shadows. Socrates wants us to see that the forms are the real causes of the "shadows" we see around us. He is also warning us that most people want to return to the warmth and comfort of the cave; philosophy can be difficult, but if we stick with it our philosophical eyes will become accustomed to the brightness of truth.

What did Plato mean by "true cause"? He had two thoughts. The first was that scientific explanations always seem somehow incomplete, and the second was that there were higher or better explanations to be had. Consider this example: Ernie is a 6-year-old boy who is known for two things: He always tells the truth and he loves to learn things. Now, Ernie is not allowed to watch Channel X on television, because it only comes on after his bedtime. But, one night Ernie's father comes downstairs at 2 a.m. and finds Ernie watching Channel X. He yells, "Why are you sitting there watching that garbage on the television?" Ernie says, "Well, Dad, I'm sitting here because gravity prohibits levitation, and as for what I am watching, some years ago not very good actors performed in front of a camera, which then recorded the performance on tape. That tape is now being played in a studio in Los Angeles, which then beams the signal to a satellite using microwave radiation. The satellite then beams the signal to our cable company that then sends an electromagnetic signal to the cathode ray tube in the back of the TV. Ambient light in the room then reflects off of the screen of the TV, and imprints an image on the back of my eye. Rods and cones in the back of the eye then send an image up the optic nerve to my brain, where certain neurons are stimulated, making it seem as if I am seeing those bad actors from a few years ago."

Now, what happens to Ernie as he gives this answer we will leave to your imagination, but note that he told the truth. He answered the "why?" question with scientific facts. But, he answered the wrong "why?" question. Ernie's dad wanted to know his intention, his purpose, and why Ernie thought it was better to break the rules of the house. Note that whenever we ask why someone does something, there are always two possible, and different, true answers. We can give the physical cause and we can give what we might call the *purposive* cause. For example, you are asked why you are sitting in the classroom, you can truly say that your bones and muscles enabled you to walk into the room and sit down. But, you can also say that you decided that it was better (for whatever reason) for you to show up at school today. It doesn't matter whether you are in school because you want to learn, or because you are afraid of being punished if you cut, the point is that you freely chose to be here; you judged that it was the best thing to do.

Now, this makes sense when we are asking about human actions. In this case, the true causes are found by finding out why someone thought that a particular action was the best one in the circumstances. Plato thought that we should also try to find true causes for all events. In addition to finding out the physical cause of the Moon orbiting the Earth, we should ask why it is better that it does so. We should assume that the physical world somehow reflects the perfection of the world of abstract ideas and seek the true causes of beauty and goodness. This may seem strange to us, living as we do in a world dominated by scientific explanations, but Plato believed that all science begins with philosophy.

APPENDIX C

Empiricism

(For use with Chapter 2)

In Chapter 2, we learned that the Scottish philosopher David Hume believed that all of our knowledge comes from experience. Apart from some basic instincts, nothing is innate. This belief is the hallmark of a philosophical view known as *empiricism*. Empiricism comes from a Greek word that means experience, and one classic definition of empiricism is this: Experience is the one and only source of information about the world. Another classic definition can be found in the work of the philosopher John Locke, whom we encounter in Chapter 12. He says that when we are born, our minds are like blank slates (in Latin, this is called *tabula rasa*). Slate is the material that blackboards were once made of, so Locke is saying that at birth our minds are clean blackboards, and all of the information we obtain after birth is written on that board by sense experience.

There have been empiricist philosophers throughout history, but most people associate empiricism with a trio of British philosophers who lived in the 17th and 18th centuries: John Locke, George Berkeley, and David Hume. We have seen that Hume has important views about ethics and art, and we will see that Locke has important views about politics—he was a great influence on the composition of the United States Constitution. All three philosophers also had important views about science (remember that science, as we know it today, was only just emerging when these men lived).

George Berkeley was born in Ireland, where he became Bishop of Cloyne. He wrote an important book on optics and vision, but he is most famous for his almost paradoxical version of empiricism. He claims that even though all of our ideas must come from experience; it is not matter in the external world that causes them. Rather, our ideas come directly from God, and matter, Berkeley says, does not exist. Berkeley later lived for 3 years in Newport, RI. At a time when slavery was still practiced in the Americas, Berkeley was promised money to start a college in Bermuda for African and Native Americans. The promised money never arrived.

Why are some philosophers attracted to empiricism? John Locke was reacting to the view, held by Plato and many others, that some knowledge is innate; that when we are born some knowledge is already in us. One contemporary of Locke, Réne Descartes, went so far as to say that the ideas of complex mathematics, and of the existence of God, were with us from birth. But, Locke countered that if this is true, we should expect young children to be great mathematicians. And, in most cases, this is just not true. It is worth noting that in his political philosophy, Locke is committed to equality, and empiricism seems to be a philosophical position that is committed to equality when it comes to knowledge.

David Hume offered two arguments *for* empiricism. We can call the first Hume's Challenge. Hume said: Take any idea that you can think of and try to trace it to your experiences. He bet that we can trace it to some set of experiences we have had (he used the term *impressions*). He gave as an example the idea of a mountain of gold, which of course does not exist. He said that we can form this idea from our ideas of mountains and of gold—we have all seen pictures of each of these. Try taking Hume's challenge now. Try to think of an idea that does not come from sense experience or some combination of experiences.

Infinity

Réne Descartes was no empiricist. He thought that there was at least one idea that he could have neither made up nor derived from experience. That idea is God, conceived as infinitely wise and powerful. It is the concept of infinity that is driving the claim here. Descartes is almost certainly correct that the idea of infinity cannot come directly from experience, for everything we experience is finite. But, is he correct that we cannot have made it up? Hume would claim that to get the idea of an infinitely long line we need only start with a finite length, mentally double it, and understand that we can keep doubling it indefinitely. Do you think that this is sufficient to explain our idea of an infinitely long line? Descartes called this only a "negative" conception of infinity, implying that we have a more powerful "positive" conception. Do you think that we do?

Some will think that the idea of God is one idea that cannot come from sense experience. Hume anticipated this objection, and argues that our idea of God simply comes from us reflecting on our own good qualities, such as charity, and amplifying them without limit.

The second argument for empiricism makes for a good thought experiment (it is called the Molyneux problem). Imagine that someone who has been blind from birth will suddenly regain sight. This person will have learned, by touch, how to tell the difference between a cotton ball and a pot-scrubber, or between a cube and a sphere. The sightless person has learned to name these objects by touch alone. So, imagine that these four items are placed on a table in front of the person who has her sight restored. Before touching the four items, will she be able to tell which is which? Empiricists will argue that she could not. What do you think? And, here is a tough challenge: Can you design an experiment that would test the empiricists' claim? (Hint: Think about the look of orange juice and grapefruit juice, or a cola and a clear citrus soda. Now think of the taste of each of these pairs.)

It is no accident that empiricism arose as a popular philosophical stance when modern science was maturing just a few hundred years ago. After all, experience and evidence is what drives science. So, in many ways, we are all allied with empiricism today, because science plays such a dominant role in our society. And, we cannot afford to ignore science. But, we also need to ask whether science is the only source of meaning in our lives.

GLOSSARY

abstract ideas—objects of thought that have no physical form

affirmative action—requires businesses and universities to ensure that oppressed groups enjoy the same opportunities as everyone else

agnostics—people who believe that we can never attain adequate answers to profound questions such as the existence of God or the meaning of life

anarchist—someone who advocates a society without any government

atheists—those who assert that there is no such thing as God

bioethics—the philosophical study of ethical issues connected with the biological sciences, particularly medicine

category mistake—describes something as the wrong kind of thing

contradiction—when you both assert and deny the same thing

counterfactual conditionals—say that if the world were different than it is, then certain things would be true

deontology—a morality based on rights and duties

discrimination—a kind of mistreatment; happens when someone makes you feel inferior or denies you equal rights because you belong to a certain group

environmentalist—someone who tries to conserve and recycle rather than polluting and endangering nature

essence—what you really are deep down inside

existence—what you do throughout your life

existentialism—the view that free choice is the defining characteristic of human existence

expressionism—this view holds that the purpose of art is to express the artist's innermost thought and feelings

factory farming—the standard way of producing meat, poultry, and milk products today

false presupposition—when someone assumes something that isn't true

genetic engineering—science that studies the microscopic structure of living tissue

hedonism—this view advocates living life to the fullest without regard for conventional morality

irrational—something is irrational if there is no reason for it

limited use position—before being allowed to do an experiment, a scientist must show that the potential benefit will realistically outweigh the harm to the subjects

metaphysical—something that transcends reality (it literally means "beyond science")

nihilist—someone who does not believe that life is meaningful

objectivism—this view holds that statements about beauty are matters of fact

oppression—the debilitating effect of discrimination; keeps someone down and prevents them from achieving happiness and success

paradox—a situation that looks normal on the surface, but when you look deeper, you find a contradiction that makes the situation impossible

possible world—an imaginary life, related to real life, but having some salient differences

pragmatism—the view that is concerned with unanswerable questions

problem of suffering (also known as the problem of evil)—the question of whether there is a way to reconcile the terrible pain in this world with the existence of God

rational—something is rational if there are reasons for it

relativism—the view that there is no such thing as a single truth for everyone

religious skepticism—the view that the existence of so much suffering in the world indicates that God does not exist

representationalism—this view holds that art should imitate or represent nature

social contract theorist—someone who holds that government is created and legitimized by a contract or agreement among the relevant parties

state of nature—the (fictional) state of affairs before any government

stoicism—the view that a person should accept everything that happens without any emotion

subjectivism—this view holds that when we make a statement about beauty, we are reporting a personal reaction, not a matter of fact

theists—those who believe in the existence of God

theodicy—justification of God

utilitarianism—centered on the idea that the moral worth of an action depends on its consequences

ABOUT THE AUTHORS

For the past several years, Sharon Kaye and Paul Thomson have been teaching philosophy to high school students through the Carroll-Cleveland Philosophers' Program, which won the 2006 American Philosophical Association Award for Excellence and Innovation in Philosophy Programs. This textbook grew out of their experience with the Carroll-Cleveland Philosophers and they continue to use it in the classroom each year. The authors have presented the drama pedagogy it employs at academic conferences in Chicago; San Francisco; Manchester College, Oxford; New College, Cambridge; New College, Oxford; Toronto; and at the University of Strathclyde in Glasgow, Scotland.

Sharon Kaye received her Ph.D. at the University of Toronto in 1997. She currently serves as an associate professor at John Carroll University, teaching philosophy of education, philosophy of friendship, metaphysics, and medieval philosophy, among other courses. She has published widely on various topics including *On Augustine* (2001), with Paul Thomson. She is also the faculty adviser for the campus chapter of Amnesty International.

Paul Thomson received his Ph.D. at Princeton University in 1990. He currently serves as an associate professor at John Carroll University, teaching and publishing in epistemology, philosophy of science, and early modern philosophy. He is also past director of John Carroll's First Year Seminar.